Questions, Questioning Techniques, and Effective Teaching

Questions, Questioning Techniques, and Effective Teaching

William W. Wilen, Editor

Produced in cooperation with
the NEA Mastery In Learning Project

nea PROFESSIONAL LIBRARY
National Education Association
Washington, D.C.

Note

The opinions expressed in this publication should not be construed as representing the policy or position of the National Education Association. Materials published as part of the Aspects of Learning series are intended to be discussion documents for teachers who are concerned with specialized interests of the profession.

Library of Congress Cataloging-in-Publication Data

Questions, questioning techniques, and effective teaching.

(Aspects of Learning)
"Produced in cooperation with NEA Mastery in Learning Project."
1. Teaching.   2. Questioning.   I. Wilen, William W.
II. Series.
LB1027.44.Q47 1987   371.1'02   87-14112
ISBN 0-8106-1484-7
ISBN 0-8106-1485-5 (pbk.)   ®‹⟨₨₍₣ᵢₗₑₛ⟩⟩3

CONTENTS

The Editor

William W. Wilen is Associate Professor of Education, Department of Teacher Development and Curriculum Studies, Kent State University, Ohio. He is also the author of *Questioning Skills, for Teachers*, published by NEA.

The Advisory Panel

David Bell, Director of Teacher Education, Arkansas College, Batesville

Beatrice C. Boyles, retired elementary school principal, Wilmington, Delaware

Earl D. Clark, Director, Clark Group: Practice into Theory, Juneau, Alaska

Libby G. Cohen, Associate Professor, College of Education, University of Southern Maine, Gorham

William K. Esler, Professor, Educational Foundations, University of Central Florida, Orlando

Liz Kebric, former Language Arts Department Head, Clear Creek Independent School District, Houston, Texas

Tedd Levy, Social Studies teacher. Nathan Hale Middle School. Norwalk, Connecticut

Donald O. Schneider, Professor and Head, Social Science Education, University of Georgia, Athens

B. Jean Stackhouse, first grade teacher, George Washington Elementary School, Durant, Oklahoma

Doug Tuthill, Philosophy and Psychology teacher, St. Petersburg High School, Florida

Allen R. Warner, Department of Curriculum and Instruction, University of Houston, Texas

Daria Portray Winter, Instructor of English Studies, University of the District of Columbia, Washington

PREFACE

Questioning is the essential component of many instructional methods including, of course, discussion and recitation. The influence of teachers' questions in the classroom is well documented by research and experience. In many respects, the primary effectiveness of the teacher lies in his or her ability to stimulate and guide students' thinking and involvement in classroom interaction related to topics, issues, and problems. The types of questions that elementary and secondary school teachers ask and the techniques and strategies they employ can make the difference between reflective, active learners and parroting, passive learners.

This book includes information that inquiring teachers want about the questions they ask and the way they ask them in their classrooms. The following specific questions are addressed:

- Why are teachers' questions and questioning practices so influential in the classroom?

- What does research say to teachers about their use of questions?

- How can questioning practices in the disciplines other than education help inform teachers about their use of questions?

- What are the cognitive and affective levels of teachers' questions and how do they relate to student learning?

- Why is the questioning technique of wait time so influential in classroom interaction?

- Which questioning techniques have been demonstrated to maximize student achievement?

- What questioning strategies are effective in stimulating students' thinking and involvement?

- What role can students' questions have in the learning process and how can they be stimulated?

- How can preservice and inservice teachers improve their questions and questioning techniques?

Questions, Questioning Techniques, and Effective Teaching is a comprehensive and authoritative resource with answers to these questions and much more. It can serve both as an information source on many aspects of teachers' questions and questioning and as a reference for trouble-shooting instructional problems related to classroom interaction. In addition, it can be used to plan inservice programs, to devise skill-development activities as part of a training program, to observe and analyze teaching, to design and revise courses of study, and to plan for instructional improvement. As such it will appeal to teachers, supervisors, administrators, researchers, educators, and students interested in instructional improvement.

This book grew out of the commitment the National Education Association has to provide teachers with materials that are useful for assisting in the improvement of instruction. One of their targeted instructional areas is teachers' questions and questioning practices. The book is dedicated to all those who value the challenge of raising and answering questions they have about their own and others' classroom questioning behaviors.

—William W. Wilen

1. WHY QUESTIONS?

by Ambrose A. Clegg, Jr., Professor of Education, Kent State University, Ohio

Consultant: James Campbell, Program Specialist, Calgary Board of Education, Canada

Teachers use questions more than any other activity. They are central to such strategies as recitation, review, discussion, inquiry, and problem solving. Current TV game and host talk shows present interesting comparisons with classroom questioning. The early research on questioning dealt with many types of questions and related them to several different classification systems. Process-product studies conducted in urban classrooms in the 1970s established sound relationships between teacher questioning and student achievement. Recent sociolinguistic studies have focused on the social context of classroom discourse and have raised new perspectives not addressed in earlier research. Future research should focus on questioning in more complex teaching situations and on the social context of student-directed discussions.

WHY QUESTIONS?

Some of the most popular television programs today are the fast-paced question and answer game shows. Enthusiasm runs high as the contestants select a category and the television host asks a series of questions—easy and obvious ones at first, more difficult and obscure ones to follow. Excitement mounts as contestants vie with one another to win glamorous prizes, only to lose it all when they are stumped on a deliberately tough question. Or if luck (and a keen memory) is with

11

them, they may win thousands of dollars in prize money and return for several successive weeks in a long winning streak.

Equally popular are the host/interview talk shows. Phil Donahue, Charlie Rose, and recently Oprah Winfrey, all have enormous popularity and high ratings. In each case, the host skillfully uses a variety of questioning formats to interview a guest, a panel of experts, and a studio or phone-in audience. Almost always the audience is held spellbound for an hour.

What is the fascination with these game and talk shows? Why are they so popular? And what do they have to tell us about the use of questions in the school classroom?

To be sure, glamorous and expensive prizes are an attractive lure, but equally important is the carefully staged buildup of excitement, suspense, and good feeling for both the winners and the losers. Even locally produced versions of "Academic Challenge" by teams from area high schools often sustain high interest and enthusiasm for an entire semester without expensive prizes as the principal incentive. And using a somewhat different format, the many versions of Trivial Pursuit have added a new enthusiasm and excitement to the traditional parlor game for adults and children alike. In many ways these programs and games centered on questioning are not much different from the teaching strategies used to review prior teaching, to assess current learning, or to test broad areas of achievement. Indeed, many teachers use classroom methods that are very similar to these game show formats.

The TV host/interviews also involve many aspects of good teaching. Not only do they probe deeply with carefully prepared questions that elicit important information, but the host also skillfully manages the discussion by asking questions that bring out a variety of viewpoints and that tap feelings, emotions, and values. It is not unusual for participants or members of the audience to be moved to such varied emotional reactions as laughter, anger, sympathy, disgust, or compassion during the hour-long programs. But perhaps the most important characteristic of these shows is that the host remains nonjudgmental about the participants' responses and does not evaluate or grade them as good or bad, pass or fail, but instead provides supportive encouragement for the speaker to expand in greater detail or feeling. While the comparisons with classroom teaching are not exact, and the goals of the schools are related to student learning and not to entertainment, there is much we can learn from such TV programs that can enhance our knowledge of the use of questioning as a teaching strategy (Passe 1984).

THE IMPORTANCE OF QUESTIONING

Of the many techniques of teaching, questioning is by far the one most commonly used at all grade levels. One recent study indicated that teachers ask as many as 300 to 400 questions a day (Levin and Long 1981). They also tend to ask them in rapid-fire fashion. Teachers in third grade reading groups asked a question every 43 seconds (Gambrell 1983) and teachers in junior high English classes averaged as many as five questions a minute (Hoetker and Ahlbrand 1969).

Teachers have long used questioning strategies to review, to check on learning, to probe thought processes, to pose problems, to seek out different or alternative solutions, and to challenge students to reflect on critical issues or values they had not previously considered. Hilda Taba (1966) described questions as "the single most influential teaching act" because of the power of questions to impact student thinking and learning. As Taba pointed out, the form of the teacher's question signals the student as to the expected level of response, thus controlling the student thought or response pattern. For example, when the teacher asks the student for the names of Columbus's three ships, this calls for only the recall of previously learned information. In contrast, if the class were studying the roles of various delegates to the Constitutional Convention and the teacher asked one student, "Would you vote to approve the constitution? How would you defend your position?" this would be an open-ended question that would allow the student to formulate a response in a number of possible ways with varying levels of thought process, all of which could be appropriate responses. There is now a growing body of evidence reviewed extensively by Brophy and Good (1986) and by Wilen and Clegg (1986) that demonstrates that appropriate questions, properly asked, contribute to significant improvement in student learning. Also, the advent of videotape recorders in many schools now makes it much easier for teachers to observe their own teaching behaviors, to reflect critically upon their questioning practices, and to practice successful models demonstrated during inservice programs. Much of this current research on student achievement and teacher development is summarized in later chapters in this book.

RENEWED INTEREST IN CLASSROOM QUESTIONS

The current interest in classroom questions is not something entirely new. Indeed, one of the most enduring models of the art of questioning dates back to the time of Plato and Socrates in 335 B.C. In the book, *Meno*, Plato describes a dialog between Socrates and a young student named Meno, dealing with the question of whether virtue could be taught. To illustrate Plato's concept that knowledge is the recall of some hidden insight or preexisting form, Socrates engages in an extended question and answer dialog about the geometry of squares with Meno's slave boy. The key to this dialog is Socrates' use of leading questions, and his technique of using the boy's answers to develop inferences and deductions from them. This led to more leading questions and to hypotheses ("if this is so, then it must follow that ...") to test the knowledge in new situations. This ancient model of teaching has been called the Socratic dialog and was used throughout the Middle Ages as the principal mode of teaching in the universities. Even today, this questioning dialog is used extensively in law schools to help students think through the application of certain legal principles to specific cases, as John Houseman demonstrated so superbly in the weekly TV episodes of "Paper Chase."

Early in the twentieth century Stevens (1912) studied methods of teaching and found that questioning, especially in the recitation form, was the most common teaching activity at all grade levels, but particularly so in the elementary schools. It was not until Bloom (1956) developed a taxonomy of educational objectives based on a hierarchy of cognitive processes that researchers began to see a useful way of classifying instructional goals and teaching activities. These taxonomy levels included such thought processes as knowledge, comprehension, application, analysis, synthesis, and evaluation. Sanders (1966) adapted this model by using it as a guide for identifying and describing the many types of questions that teachers ask, categorizing them at the various cognitive levels of Bloom's taxonomy. Sanders's work proved immediately useful and provided the impetus for a long series of studies that analyzed the cognitive level of classroom questioning, examined the effects of using higher-level questions upon student achievement, and provided evidence that teacher inservice training resulted in higher student performance (Pfeiffer and Davis 1965; Davis and Hunkins 1966; Davis and Tinsley 1967; Davis et al. 1969; Farley and Clegg 1970; Manson and Clegg 1970; Sebolt and Clegg 1970).

Quite a different strategy of questioning proposed by Gallagher and Aschner (1963) was based on Guilford's (1956) three-dimensional model of intellectual processes. Guilford conceived of the intellect as a complex structure of some 120 separately identifiable mental abilities. These were

14

derived from a hypothetical model that interrelated five classes of intellectual operations, with four kinds of content, with six types of thought products or outcomes. Guilford (1959) described this model in an article aptly titled, "Three Faces of Intellect."

The feature of the Guilford model that provoked the most interest related to classroom questioning was its identification of convergent and divergent thinking processes as they relate to creativity. Gallagher and Aschner's (1963) subsequent studies on creativity led them to identify five types of questions often found in teaching situations: cognitive-memory, convergent, divergent, evaluative, and routine. They defined convergent questions as those that tend to channel a student's responses along a single direction. They are usually narrowly defined and often require a single correct or best answer. Divergent questions are those that seek a variety of possible answers or solutions to a problem. They encourage creative or unusual responses rather than a single, best solution. Such questions tend to be broad and open-ended, and encourage a variety of possible answers, all of which could be acceptable. Their research, however, indicated that divergent questions, those most likely to elicit creative and high-level responses, were seldom used by classroom teachers.

To return to our earlier comparison with the TV programs, the fast-paced quiz show is built upon the convergent questioning strategy. Only a single, correct answer will win the prize or allow you to go on to the next round. Seldom is there a dispute with the host or judge about other possible answers. When there is, the host replies in teacherlike fashion, "That is not the answer I was looking for." In contrast, the Phil Donahue and Oprah Winfrey host/talk shows make much greater use of open-ended, divergent-thinking questions. The host skillfully seeks to bring out new knowledge or unorthodox viewpoints on the topic under discussion, and then quickly moves to contrast it with positions previously stated by the panel of experts or the audience. In all of this give-and-take, there are no rewards or points scored, no frenzied buildup to the grand prize, no passing or failing grades. The rewards for those who participate in the TV studio and those who watch at home are intrinsic: they have explored a topic for its own sake and seem to have enjoyed it, and they have also learned something about themselves in the process. All of this suggests that we have not given enough serious attention to the place of divergent questioning strategies in classroom instruction, nor to the larger curriculum goals and classroom settings that would foster and encourage such strategies. Perhaps we are too preoccupied with the limited goals of convergent questions and the quiz show approach to recitation, review, and drill activities.

The studies mentioned broke important ground for developing an awareness of the significance of classroom questions. Teachers became aware of the preponderance of low-level, fact-recall questions in textbooks, tests, and in their daily teaching. As new textbooks were written, authors and editors gave special attention to raising the cognitive level of questions and providing more problem situations that encouraged divergent thinking processes. Classroom observational measures were developed that combined a question classification system with a matrix or grid for recording and analyzing the pattern of teacher questions and student answers in the context of classroom discussions or recitations. Other researchers began to tape-record and transcribe extended segments of dialog to search for teachers' verbal clues that seemed to elicit higher-level responses from students, or that acted to inhibit or discourage student responses. Clegg (1971) summarized the efforts of this period to translate a rapidly growing body of theory and research into classroom applications.

QUESTIONS AND EFFECTIVE TEACHING

With all this new emphasis upon teacher questions, was there any evidence that it paid off in long-term student gains? Much of the data was fragmentary and conflicting, and advocates of one system or another of teacher questioning were often long on ideological commitment to a favorite theory and short on clear and convincing evidence of student gains.

The emphasis of research studies took a major turn in the early 1970s, however, as Congress began to demand answers to whether the millions that were being spent on Head Start and Follow Through programs resulted in any significant educational gains for poor and minority students. More specifically, gains were defined almost exclusively in terms of increases in student achievement on standardized tests of basic skills in reading, writing, and mathematics. In response, the Office of Education and the newly created National Institute of Education embarked on a series of long-term, carefully designed evaluation (and later research) studies of Project Follow Through on a national scale never before attempted. These studies were designed on a model called "process-product" research that asked the basic question: Is there a

16

relationship between certain teaching behaviors (process), such as the use of various types of teacher questions, and specific student achievement outcomes (products)? This model was controversial, of course, since it dealt only with measured achievement in school subjects, and ignored the broader social and personal goals of schooling. Nevertheless, for the first time it took advantage of a large wealth of data from scores of classrooms in major urban cities.

The research focused around a sequence of the following three questions:

1. Can we observe and describe the teaching behavior in some systematic way?
2. If so, is there a statistical correlation between the teaching behavior and the student outcome that permits some meaningful interpretation of the relationship?
3. Can we demonstrate, in carefully designed classroom experiments, that the specific behavior does indeed produce the desired outcome of increased student achievement?

This paradigm is called the descriptive-correlational-experimental research loop (Gage 1978; Rosenshine and Furst 1973).

The results of nearly a decade of this process-product research are presented in a thorough and comprehensive review by Brophy and Good (1986). These findings, not surprisingly, indicate that teaching is a complex set of decisions and actions that are made within the social setting of the classroom and that vary on the basis of the age, maturity, and socioeconomic status (SES) of the students as well as with the specific purpose of a lesson and the level of simplicity or abstraction of the content material. Furthermore, many of the teacher behaviors studied, such as the use of high- or low-level questions, convergent or divergent thinking, the length of time a teacher waits for an answer from a student, and the type of feedback that a teacher gives when the student responds, do not have direct relationships to achievement that are consistent for all pupils. Rather, the relationships vary with grade level, SES, the complexity of content matter, and lesson goal. Wilen and Clegg (1986) identified 11 effective questioning practices that are correlated positively to student achievement but which must be used selectively by teachers depending on the classroom setting. Several chapters in this book deal extensively with the findings of process-product research, the many different effects of "wait time," and inservice programs that help teachers improve their use of effective questions.

17

QUESTIONS AS CLASSROOM DISCOURSE

The sociolinguistic analysis of classroom discourse is a wholly different approach to the study of classroom questions. Since spoken language is the medium in which much of teaching takes place, the study of classroom discourse is the study of the communication system, the rules and conventions by which it operates, and how students learn to function within it. The questions teachers ask and the ways that students respond (or choose not to) are a large part of the communication system that operates in the social and cultural context of the classroom. In short, speech unites the cognitive and the social (Cazden 1986).

Sociolinguistic research has had a long tradition in anthropology and sociology but has only recently made a major impact in education. Comprehensive reviews of the research by Green (1983) and Cazden (1986) identified not only important studies, but suggested newer methods of analysis and different conceptual approaches that are reflected in the British literature. Cazden raised serious objection to much of the process-product research discussed above, arguing that counting and analyzing discrete teacher behaviors misses much of the social context in which the intent and meaning of language is established. She pointed out that questions are closed or open-ended only in the context of what came before and during previous instruction and what the teacher or students do next in response. For example, suppose a teacher asks a question that calls for a creative response such as: "How do you explain the contradiction that the same Thomas Jefferson who wrote, 'All men are created equal,' continued to own slaves on his plantation at Monticello until his death?" The initial response calls for high-level analysis, evaluation, and creative synthesis. But if the same question is asked several days later on a test, it is then reduced to a low-level recall question. Similar problems are involved in following up complex higher-level questions with a single student in the course of a group lesson. Did the student respond at a high-cognitive level on his or her own initiative, or in response to contextual cues supplied by the teacher or other students (Cazden 1986, p. 452)?

While the sociolinguistic approach has not yielded the type of generalizations related to achievement identified by Wilen and Clegg (1986), it has raised other issues that should provoke thoughtful analyses of teacher and student questions within a framework of "cognition in social context." Consider, for example, that the formal structure of the classroom represents the norms and values of the teacher, not those of the students. This is especially true where children come from different ethnic, cultural, or SES groups than the teacher. Whereas these students can converse in vital and enthusiastic language at home or in the streets, they often fall silent in the classroom.

Working in rural Black and white communities, Heath (1982) found that the form and function of questions asked by parents in the home differed from those asked by teachers in the schools; achievement improved when teachers modified their questioning strategies to be more like those in the home.

In an early education program for Polynesian children in Hawaii, researchers found that when the ways in which children participated in group reading lessons were simplified and made more like those in the family structure, children paid more attention to the academic task (Au 1980).

Finally, we might consider the role of language in the unofficial peer culture, where the student, not the teacher is the expert. Students use very different language patterns when tutoring other students. They ask fewer questions and spend more time clarifying and explaining specific difficulties. In classes using microcomputers, it is often the students who have more expertise than the teacher, but they share the knowledge willingly and enthusiastically and do not resort to authoritarian or punitive behaviors to control access to knowledge.

At the microlevel, there is a well-developed system that defines how people are governed by language usage. The classroom has a well-defined, if not always public, set of rules that determine who speaks when, to whom, how (openly or in secret whispers), and for how long. Students learn to recognize the meaning of different intonations and words such as "right now," or the use of a soft voice as a signal to pay attention when giving directions. Cazden (1986) has pointed out that teachers in primary grades often use a patronizing form of baby talk and refer to themselves in a curious, impersonal way. "Mrs. Jones wouldn't like that, would she?" Formal control is asserted by establishing a social distance from students, using politeness, courtesy and formal titles of address, and generally avoiding humor, affect, or feeling, especially in the upper grades. Goodlad's study (1983) of more than 1,000 classrooms found that affect, either positive or negative, was virtually absent and that schools could be described only as neutral or flat (p. 467).

In summary, the sociolinguistic approach has opened the door to much more intensive analysis of classroom discourse. From this perspective, we know very little about the impact of teacher questions, the types that may be more effective in differing social contexts, or the social interactions between teachers and students that enhance or inhibit the use of questions during teaching. The examples of research studies cited, however, should be instructive and cause us to reexamine old issues within this new framework.

FUTURE DIRECTIONS

Most of the studies discussed above dealt with a limited array of questioning techniques; effectiveness has often been tied to the criterion of measurable results on standardized tests. But there is still a larger domain of questioning that has not been adequately studied. This includes the more complex cognitive thinking tasks of conceptualizing, generalizing, and hypothesizing, as well as those open-ended questions that seek creative solutions or multiple responses to problem solving. Another underexamined area is analysis, in which probing questions may help students identify competing value elements in important political, economic, or social issues.

Little research has been devoted to the role of student questioning. Most of the studies cited focused on a typical format of teacher question and student response, a teacher-dominated strategy. What happens when students take charge of the strategy in group-oriented discussions and control both the type of questions asked and the data bank of answers? Many content areas such as social studies, language arts, and science claim to place a high premium upon group discussion, but there is little evidence that such discussions lead to high levels of independent thinking, critical analyses of previous students' statements, creative approaches to new issues, or divergent solutions to problems. Such classroom discussions, valuable as they may be, are seldom evaluated objectively, nor are they incorporated into the current models of standardized tests. Student-directed questioning strategies in classroom discussions, such as those suggested by Francis P. Hunkins in Chapter 8, are a potentially fruitful and needed area of future research.

In short, the previous research on classroom questioning has provided data on those approaches that appear to be most effective in rather traditional classroom settings. The challenge now is to study more intensely those questioning strategies that lead to higher-order thinking, to value analysis, to creative responses to new situations, and to independent thinking in student-directed discussions.

REFERENCES

Au, K. "Participation Structures with Hawaiian Children: Analysis of a Culturally Appropriate Instructional Event." *Anthropology and Education Quarterly* 11 (1980): 91-115.

Bloom, B. S., et al., eds. *Taxonomy of Educational Objectives, Handbook I: Cognitive Domain*. New York: David McKay, 1956.

Brophy, G., and Good, T. "Teacher Behavior and Student Behavior." In *Handbook of Research on Teaching*, edited by M. Wittrock. 3d ed. New York: Macmillan, 1986.

Cazden, C. "Classroom Discourse." In *Handbook of Research on Teaching*, edited by M. Wittrock. 3d ed. New York: Macmillan, 1986.

Clegg, A. "Classroom Questions: Theory, Research and Application." In *Encyclopedia of Education*, 1971, pp. 183-90.

Davis, O., and Hunkins, F. "Textbook Questions: What Thinking Processes Do They Foster?" *Peabody Journal of Education* 43 (1966): 285-92.

Davis, O.; Morse, K.; Rogers, V.; and Tinsley, D. "Studying the Cognitive Emphasis of Teacher's Classroom Questions." *Educational Leadership* 26 (1969): 711-19.

Davis, O., and Tinsley, D. "Cognitive Questions Revealed By Classroom Questions Asked by Social Studies Student Teachers." *Peabody Journal of Education* 45 (1967): 21-26.

Farley, G., and Clegg, A. "Increasing the Cognitive Level of Classroom Questions in Social Studies" Paper presented at the meeting of the American Educational Research Association, Los Angeles, 1970. ERIC Document Reproduction Service No. ED 034-732.

Gage, N. *The Scientific Basis of the Art of Teaching*. New York: Teachers College Press, 1978.

Gallagher, J., and Aschner, M. "A Preliminary Report on Analyses of Classroom Interaction." *Merrill-Palmer Quarterly* 3 (1963): 183-94.

Gambrell, L. B. "The Occurrence of Think-Time During Reading Comprehension." *Journal of Educational Research* 75 (1983): 144-48.

Goodlad, J. "A Study of Schooling: Some Findings and Hypotheses." *Phi Delta Kappan* 64 (1983): 465-70.

Green. J. "Research in Teaching as a Linguistic Process: State of the Art." In *Review of Research In Education*, edited by E. Gordon. Vol. 10. Washington, D.C.: American Educational Research Association, 1983.

Guilford, J. "The Structure of Intellect." *Psychological Bulletin* 53 (1956): 267-93.

_____. "Three Faces of Intellect." *American Psychologist* 14 (1959): 469-79.

Heath, S. "Questioning at Home and at School: A Comparative Study." In *Doing Ethnography in Schooling: Educational Ethnography in Action*, edited by G. Spindler. New York: Holt, Rinehart and Winston, 1982.

Hoetker, J., and Ahlbrand, W. "The Persistence of the Recitation." *American Educational Research Journal* 6 (1969): 145-67.

Hunkins, F. "The Influence of Analysis and Evaluation Questions on Achievement in Sixth-Grade Social Studies." *Educational Leadership* 25 (1968): 326-32.

Levin, T., and Long, R. *Effective Instruction*. Washington, D.C.: Association for Supervision and Curriculum Development, 1981.

Manson, G., and Clegg, A. "Classroom Questions: Keys to Children's Thinking" *Peabody Journal of Education* 47 (1970): 302-7.

Passe, J. "Phil Donahue: An Excellent Model for Leading a Discussion." *Journal of Teacher Education* 35 (1984): 43-48.

Pfeiffer, I., and Davis, O. L., Jr. "Teacher-Made Examinations: What Kinds of Thinking Do They Demand?" *NASSP Bulletin* 49 (1965): 1-10.

Rosenshine, B., and Furst, N. "The Use of Direct Observation to Study Teaching." In *Second Handbook of Research on Teaching*, edited by R. W. Travers. Chicago: Rand McNally, 1973.

Sanders, N. *Classroom Questions: What Kinds?* New York: Harper and Row, 1966.

Sebolt A., and Clegg, A. "Construction of a Test for Concept Learning and Identification of the Cognitive Processes Required." Sturbridge, Mass.: Resource Learning Laboratory, Title III-PACE, 1970. ERIC Document Reproduction Service No. ED 040 892.

Stevens, R. *The Question as a Means of Efficiency in Instruction: A Critical Study of Classroom Practice*. New York: Teachers College Press, 1912.

Taba, H. *Teaching Strategies and Cognitive Functioning in Elementary School Children*. Cooperative Research Project No. 2404. San Francisco: San Francisco State College, 1966.

Wilen, W., and Clegg, A. "Effective Questions and Questioning: A Research Review." *Theory and Research in Social Education* 14 (1986): 153-61.

2. REVIEW OF RESEARCH ON QUESTIONING TECHNIQUES

by Meredith D. Gall, Professor of Education; and Tom Rhody, Graduate Teaching Fellow, College of Education, University of Oregon, Eugene

Consultants: Elizabeth M. Manibusan, Assistant Principal for Curriculum, Simon Sanchez High School, Yigo, Guam; and J. T. Dillon, Associate Professor of Education, University of California, Riverside.

Research on questions and questioning has produced findings that help us understand more about classroom interaction. Research related to six primary areas of attention is examined: question-asking and student learning; questions before, during, and after instruction; types of effective questions; techniques to help students give good answers to questions; training to improve teacher questioning; and training students to answer and ask questions. Recommendations to teachers are also made.

INTRODUCTION

Teachers have been described as "professional question-askers" (Aschner 1961). The same label might be applied to researchers. Their research is often initiated by a question they wish to answer. As their research progresses, new questions arise and lead to further investigations.

What questions have researchers asked about questions? The following six questions were found in this review of published investigations:

1. Does question-asking improve student learning?

2. Is it more effective to ask questions before, during, or after instruction?

3. What kinds of questions are most effective?

4. What techniques help students give good answers to questions?

5. Does training improve teachers' ability to ask questions?

6. Is it helpful to train students in question-answering and question-generating skills?

Each of these questions is answered in a separate section of this chapter.

Most of the research reviewed concerns the effectiveness of questioning techniques. The criterion of effectiveness in research on questions is usually student achievement on a test—often a standardized achievement test or a test specially developed by the experimenter. In a few studies, the criterion is the quality of students' oral responses to questions. Other important criteria, such as student attitudes, language development, or ability to engage in inquiry, rarely have been used in questioning research. Therefore, when this review concludes that a particular questioning practice is effective, it is because the practice improves either students' performance on an achievement test or the quality of their oral responses.

This review focuses primarily on questions that teachers ask during classroom instruction. When appropriate, however, research on questions in textbooks, tests, and homework is reviewed.

Researchers have investigated certain aspects of question-asking more than others; therefore, those findings that are well established as well as those that are tentative are indicated.

In the chapter conclusion, implications of the findings for classroom teachers who want to improve their questioning skills are explored.

DOES QUESTION-ASKING IMPROVE STUDENT LEARNING?

Asking Questions Is Effective

Most teachers assume that asking questions contributes to the effectiveness of their instruction. Research supports this assumption. For example, Gall et al. (1978) conducted an experiment in which some elementary school classes studied a two-week unit on ecology in which

24

they read a textbook assignment each day and then answered the teacher's questions about it. Other classes of students read the same assignment but then engaged in an ecology-related art activity that did not involve questions. The students who participated in the question-and-answer session did better than the other students on a variety of achievement tests administered at the end of the experiment. Similar results demonstrating the superiority of instruction using questions to instruction without questions was found by Eddinger (1985).

Similar studies have been done using "inserted questions." In this research, experimenters insert questions of different types at various places in reading passages to observe their effects. Frase (1967) compared the effectiveness of having some students read passages without inserted questions, while other students read the same passages and also responded to inserted questions. The latter group of students did better on a subsequent test assessing their mastery of the reading passages.

Although both oral and written questions promote student learning, at least one study (Hargie 1978) found that oral questions are more effective. This may be because the modalities of *listening* to teachers' questions and answering by *speaking* are easier for many students than *reading* textbook questions and *writing* answers to them.

Questions, then, are better than no questions. Also, more questions may be better than fewer questions, as Rosenshine (1986) concluded in his review of research.

Why do questions have this beneficial effect? At least seven reasons have been offered by researchers (Gall 1984; Palincsar and Brown, 1984; Wittrock, 1981):

1. Questions are motivating, and so they keep students on task.

2. Questions focus the student's attention on what is to be learned. A teacher's question is a cue to the student that the information required to answer the question is important.

3. Questions, especially thought questions, elicit depth of processing. Rather than reading the text passively, a good question requires the student to process the text actively and transform it into terms meaningful to him or her.

4. Questions activate metacognitive processes. (Metacognitions are the thoughts we have about our own learning processes.) Thus, students become aware of how well they are mastering the

curriculum content and whether they need to study it further.

5. Questions elicit further practice and rehearsal of the curriculum content.

6. If the student answers a question correctly, that is reinforcing, and the teacher may further reinforce the answer by praising or acknowledging it. If the student answers incorrectly, that can prompt the teacher to engage in reteaching.

7. Students' mastery of the curriculum is usually assessed by tests that consist of questions. Therefore, questions asked during instruction are consistent with the task requirement of tests.

Questions, then, are effective for many reasons. Research has not determined whether teachers consciously use questions for these reasons, but it has established that teachers use them frequently. In fact, teacher questions constitute a tenth to a sixth of all classroom-interaction time (Dunkin and Biddle 1974). Also, one of the most commonly used methods in elementary and secondary school teaching is recitation, which involves rapid question-and-answer exchanges orchestrated by the teacher, usually for the purpose of assessing how well students have mastered the content of a lesson. Teachers' reliance on the recitation method has been documented by researchers since the last century (Hoetker and Ahlbrand 1969), continuing up to the present day (Sirotnik 1983; Durkin 1978-79).

Questions Can Have Detrimental Effects

Questions are effective, but not under all conditions. Dillon (1981b; 1978) demonstrated that high school students actually give briefer responses to teacher questions than to teacher statements. He argued that if the teacher's objective is to stimulate thought, other methods are more effective than question-asking. These alternative methods include paraphrasing what a student has said, expressing perplexity, and inviting students to elaborate on their responses (Dillon 1981a).

Researchers (e.g., Boomer 1979) also criticized recitations because they allow teachers to monopolize the talk space and discourage open communication and language use among students. This criticism may be unfair, because it does not reflect the teacher's objectives in using

26

recitation. Recitation is effective in promoting review of curriculum content that the teacher deems important. If the teacher's objective is to stimulate student thought and language development, methods such as discussion (Gall 1985) may be more effective.

Another potentially detrimental effect of questions was found by Martin (1979). He observed that as a teacher increased the use of higher-cognitive questions, students' higher-order responses increased accordingly. Unfortunately, students also became more negative in their attitude toward the teacher. Martin speculated that the shift in attitude was caused by the greater effort required to answer the higher-cognitive questions.

Questions May Be Unnecessary

Two studies found that questions neither helped nor hindered the achievement of certain students. Wong (1979) found that questions on main ideas helped the learning of fifth-grade learning-disabled children, but not the learning of normally achieving children. Seretny and Dean (1986) found that inserted questions (questions inserted in reading assignments) improved the achievement of normal and below-average readers, but had little effect on above-average readers.

An explanation for this finding is that some students have developed their own strategies for mastering curriculum content, so that they are not dependent on questions posed by the teacher or text. For example, Garner and Alexander (1982) found that mature readers generated their own questions spontaneously as they studied a reading passage in preparation for a test.

IS IT MORE EFFECTIVE TO ASK QUESTIONS BEFORE, DURING, OR AFTER INSTRUCTION?

By *instruction*, we mean the presentation of new curriculum content to students through reading assignments, class lecture or demonstration, or other method. It was found in a review of the research that questions can be effective at *all three phases* relative to instruction: before, during, and after. The function of questions in each phase is different, however.

27

Questions After Instruction

It seems that most questions addressed to students follow instruction. These questions occur in the context of recitations, seatwork, homework, review sessions, and practice quizzes.

A teacher typically will conduct a recitation after students have finished reading a story or section of a textbook. Recitations take the form of rapid question-answer exchanges, and as indicated above, they are effective.

The teacher may also assign seatwork, which consists of questions in a workbook, textbook, or handout. Seatwork permits further rehearsal of the curriculum content. Several studies examined the effectiveness of seatwork in mathematics instruction. Generally, these studies (reviewed by Good, Grouws, and Ebmeier 1983) found that seatwork is effective if it is brief relative to the instructional phase of a lesson. An exception to this finding is a recent study (Gall et al. 1987) of high school algebra classes for students of average and high ability. Teachers whose students made high-achievement gains allocated an average of 13 minutes of the lesson for teacher-monitored seatwork, whereas teachers whose students made low-achievement gains only allocated 4 minutes for this purpose. Conversely, the teachers of high-gain classes only spent 17 minutes of the lesson on lecture and demonstration, whereas teachers of low-gain classes spent 27 minutes in this way.

The issue of how much emphasis to place on seatwork relative to instruction and recitation probably involves the independence level of the learner. Less independent students may well need more teacher-centered instruction and less independent seatwork. More independent students can profit from increased emphasis on seatwork so that they can practice independently and make use of their internalized study strategies.

Homework provides still another opportunity for teachers to have students rehearse curriculum content by answering assigned questions. Reviewers (Walberg, Paschal, and Weinstein 1985) concluded that homework is very effective in improving students' academic achievement.

Many teachers move students continuously from one unit of instruction to the next. It is effective to allocate some time in each unit to reviewing content from previous units. This review often takes the form of questions asked in class, usually at the start of the lesson. Reviews are probably most important in sequential curriculums, such as mathematics. In fact, researchers (Saxon 1982; Good et al. 1983) found that daily, weekly, and monthly reviews are effective in improving students' mathematics achievement. Questions in the form of quizzes also perform a review function, and they too are effective (McKenzie 1973).

Questions During Instruction

Teachers do not need to wait until after instruction to ask questions. They can easily interrupt a lecture or demonstration to ask a question or two to check student understanding. Similarly, questions in a textbook need not occur at the end of chapters. They can be interspersed in the text after paragraphs or sections of the chapter.

Research on mathematics instruction (Good et al. 1983; Gall et al. 1985) found that when a teacher is explaining a new procedure to students, it is effective to ask *all* students to solve a problem independently in order to check for understanding. This request is sometimes called "controlled practice," and it should occur prior to seatwork. The advantage of controlled practice is that it keeps all students on task and informs the teacher whether reteaching is necessary prior to assigning seatwork and homework. In the study of high school algebra instruction previously described (Gall et al. 1987), it was found that teachers of high-gain classes spent an average of 3.4 minutes of the lesson in controlled practice, whereas teachers of low-gain classes spent only 0.5 minutes on this activity.

The research on controlled practice, which involves questions during instruction, was done in mathematics classes. It seems likely, however, that this questioning technique would be similarly effective in other curriculum subjects involving skill development.

Questions Before Instruction

Researchers have developed a new theory to explain how reading comprehension occurs. This theory states that readers have mental schemas that allow them to assimilate new information in a text. Learners with well-developed, relevant schemas can comprehend new information in the text better than learners with less well-developed schemas.

Schema theory suggests that it would be helpful to activate students'

29

schemas *prior* to having them read text or listen to the teacher present new information. This activation process can occur by asking such questions as, "What do you already know about _____?" or "What do you think will happen in the next part of the story based on what you already know?" Two studies (Hansen 1981; Hansen and Pearson 1983) found that asking such questions improved students' comprehension of text. The questions were most helpful for poor readers.

Research on schema-activating questions is currently influencing the construction of reading comprehension tests (Rowe 1986). New tests assessing reading comprehension are being developed to include questions prior to each passage as well as the traditional questions that follow the passage. The questions prior to the passage are not answered and scored, but only serve to prepare the reader for the passage. It is not yet known whether the inclusion of schema-activating questions will improve students' performance on these tests.

WHAT TYPES OF QUESTIONS ARE MOST EFFECTIVE?

The research reviewed does not indicate that one type of question is necessarily better than another. Rather, each type of question is effective for a particular instructional objective. Therefore, teachers need to decide on their objectives for a lesson or unit, and then choose the appropriate types of questions.

Intentional Versus Incidental Questions

Teachers often end a unit of instruction with a test. If the test contains a question that also was asked before, during, or after instruction, researchers call it an *intentional* question. Otherwise, it is called an *incidental* question and it requires the student to recall information or ideas not previously rehearsed in instruction.

Not surprisingly, researchers found that students perform substantially better on intentional test items than they do on incidental test items. Hamaker (1986) reviewed 61 experiments that have been done on questions inserted in reading passages. He found that students consistently do better on both higher-cognitive and fact-test questions if they have previously encountered and answered these questions while initially reading the text material. Gall and his colleagues (1978) found the same phenomenon with teacher-led recitations with elementary students.

30

The distinction between intentional and incidental questions extends beyond the specific information or ideas tested. Hillman (1979) examined the effects of questions on learning among 90 educable mentally retarded children in the intermediate grades. Some of the students were trained to answer "remembering"-type questions while others were trained to answer "inferring"-type questions. On a criterion test containing both types of items, each group outperformed the other on the type of questions on which they had training. In other words, the emphasis on one type of question rather than on the other shaped the way the students processed the curriculum content. Wixson (1983) found a similar effect in a research project involving typical fifth-grade students.

There are at least two reasons why it is effective to ask students questions during instruction that are similar to those that will appear later on a test. First, the questions asked during instruction give students the opportunity to practice the information or thinking processes before being tested on them. Second, the teacher's questions asked during instruction cue students on the curriculum content that the teacher considers most important. By knowing the teacher's priorities, the student can devote extra study effort to those priorities. For example, McKenzie (1973) observed, "Students say they use different methods of study when they expect multiple-choice, fill-in-the-blank, and essay tests. Generally, students report attempting to memorize details and specific words for objective tests while they study general trends and form generalizations and personal opinions when preparing for essay tests" (p. 285). Indeed, books on study skills (Gall and Gall 1985) often recommend that students "figure out" the teacher and try to anticipate the questions that the teacher will ask on tests.

Is is fair to cue students in advance to what will be on a test by asking intentional questions? With younger or lower-achieving students, it seems appropriate to make explicit what you think is important for them to remember or to be able to do. Explicit instruction may not be necessary for older and higher-achieving students because they can figure out on their own what is important in the curriculum material.

Higher-Cognitive and Lower-Cognitive Questions

The most thoroughly investigated issue in questioning research is whether it is more effective for teachers to emphasize higher-cognitive questions or lower-cognitive questions in their instruction. Higher-cognitive questions are usually defined as questions that require students to use such thought processes as analyzing, problem solving, predicting, and evaluating. Lower-cognitive questions (also called fact questions) require only memory or the ability to locate information in a textbook or other source.

Winne (1979) reviewed 18 experiments on this issue and concluded that it made no difference to student learning whether the teacher emphasized higher-cognitive or lower-cognitive questions. Redfield and Rousseau (1981) reviewed essentially the same set of experiments, but reached a different conclusion, namely, that teacher emphasis on higher-cognitive questions led to more students learning than emphasis on lower-cognitive questions. This conclusion does not mean that all experiments found this effect. Indeed, some experiments found that emphasis on lower-cognitive questions was more effective. Redfield and Rousseau found only that the *majority* of the experiments favored higher-cognitive questions.

The picture is further complicated by three major studies of classroom instruction reviewed by Rosenshine (1976). He concluded that lower-cognitive questions were more effective than higher-cognitive questions in promoting student academic achievement.

Three factors that might explain why different studies produced these different results can be identified.

First, researchers tend to use different definitions of higher-cognitive questions and to study different questions. Some researchers rely on the *Taxonomy of Educational Objectives Handbook* (Bloom et al. 1956), while others use a classification system based on Guilford's structure-of-intellect model (Aschner et al. 1965). Reading researchers tend to classify questions using the three categories developed by Pearson and Johnson (1978): text-explicit questions, which can be answered directly from the text; text-implicit questions, which involve making an inference from several items of information in the text; and script-implicit questions, which require an answer that comes from students' prior knowledge. Also, higher-cognitive questions at one grade level may require quite different thought processes than higher-cognitive questions at another grade level. Interestingly, the three studies reviewed by Rosenshine involved primary grade instruction, whereas the studies reviewed by Redfield and Rousseau spanned the grades from kindergarten through high school.

The second factor is that the American school curriculum has predominantly lower-cognitive objectives (Goodlad 1983). For this reason, teachers ask mostly lower-cognitive questions in their regular instruction (Blosser 1979; Gall 1970; Hare and Pulliam 1980; Sirotnik 1983). Thus, when an experiment is done, teachers find it relatively easy to implement instruction that favors lower-cognitive questions. Teachers assigned to instruction emphasizing higher-cognitive questions must make much greater adjustments in their curriculum and teaching behavior.

The third factor that explains the inconsistent results is the type of student in the classes studied by the researcher. Higher-cognitive questions, virtually by definition, make more demands on the learner. An indication of their difficulty is reported in several studies (Dillon 1982b; Mills et al. 1980), which found that the cognitive level of students' responses is often below the cognitive level of the question posed by the teacher. If students cannot handle the cognitive demands of these questions, their learning may be hampered. Indeed, they might profit more from lower-cognitive questions on which they can be successful.

In the three studies reviewed by Rosenshine, the research was conducted in low-achieving urban schools. Children in these schools probably could better handle the response requirements of lower-cognitive questions than of higher-cognitive questions. In support of this view, Wilson (1979) found that below-average readers in sixth and seventh grade did as well as average and above-average readers on factual questions following reading passages, but did not do as well on inferential questions.

Research on the cognitive level of questions inserted in reading passages has produced more consistent results. A comprehensive review of this research (Hamaker 1986) found consistent effects favoring higher-cognitive questions. This type of question is more effective in promoting intentional and incidental higher-cognitive learning, and also possibly incidental fact learning. It is important to realize, however, that most of this research has been done on college students, who should be able to meet the demands of higher-cognitive questions.

WHAT TECHNIQUES HELP STUDENTS GIVE GOOD ANSWERS TO QUESTIONS?

It is not sufficient for teachers to ask good questions. The question also must elicit a good response from students.

This review of the research led to the identification of five effective techniques for this purpose: keeping all students on task during the question-and-answer part of the lesson; phrasing questions clearly; providing wait time; providing positive feedback to student answers; and probing student anwers to improve them.

Keep All Students on Task

An obvious limitation of recitations is that only one student at a time can answer the teacher's question. In a typical classroom of 20 to 35 students, then, each student will only be able to respond a small percentage of the time. If students are not actively responding, there is the risk that they will get off task. Researchers (Berliner and Fisher 1985) demonstrated that off-task behavior is associated with decrements in learning.

Two related experiments (McKenzie 1979; McKenzie and Henry 1979) determined whether the number of elementary students responding to a question affects their on-task behavior and achievement. The teacher in one class called on individual students to respond to questions. The teacher in the other class asked all students to respond to each question with a nonverbal gesture. For example, one of the questions was, "If you think it would rain here, raise your hand." In both experiments, the students in the whole-class response group had less off-task behavior and better performance on the final test. Furthermore, in one of the experiments the students reported feeling less anxious about taking the final test.

McKenzie's method of eliciting whole-class participation is similar to the method of "controlled practice" that was described above. Controlled practice in mathematics instruction and related subjects involves having all students work the same problem so that the teacher can check for understanding.

Many questions, however, require an oral response rather than a nonverbal or written response. What can the teacher do to ensure that all students stay on task while one student responds? Some educators recommend that teachers address their questions to the class as a whole rather than to individual students so that all students stay on their toes. Two studies of algebra instruction, however, yielded contradictory findings relating to this recommendation. Gersten et al. (1987) found that it was more effective for teachers of low-achieving algebra students to address questions to the class as a whole. Gall and his colleagues (1987), however, found that it was more effective for teachers of high-achieving algebra students to address a question to one specific student.

The best recommendation to be made at this time is for the teacher to be sensitive to the class's on-task behavior during question-and-answer exchanges, and to use whatever techniques that maintain the on-task rate at a high level. For example, it may be sufficient in some classes for teachers simply to remind students to listen carefully to their questions and to their classmates' answers.

Phrase Questions Clearly

Dillon (1986) reviewed the research on phrasing questions in several different disciplines—for example, law, psychotherapy, and education—and concluded, "... the major point about the formulation of a question is that it defines the kind of answer possible and it affects several characteristics of the eventual answer given" (p. 107). For example, if a question involves words that are unfamiliar to students, they may not be able to answer it even though they know the information being requested by the teacher.

Some teachers have the habit of asking several questions in succession before calling on a student to respond. Borg et al. (1970) found a relatively high incidence of this behavior—an average of 14 times in a 20-minute lesson—among elementary school teachers. Wright and Nuthall (1970) found that this behavior had a negative effect on student learning. The probable reason for the negative effect is that multiple questions reflect lack of clarity in the teacher's thinking and oral expression. If the teacher is unclear, it is difficult for students to give appropriate responses.

Because the phrasing of questions has an effect on student learning, teachers should consider formulating at least their major questions in advance of the lesson. It is difficult to formulate good questions spontaneously while the lesson is in progress.

Provide Wait Time

One of the early studies of classroom questioning practices (Stevens 1912) found that teachers ask a great number of questions at a high rate per minute. More recent studies have found the same pattern. Hoetker

(1986) recorded an average of five questions per minute in junior high English classes. Gambrell (1983) found that third-grade teachers asked a question every 43 seconds in their reading groups. Reviewing recent studies done in West Germany, Klinzing and Klinzing-Eurich (in press) found that teachers ask an average of nearly two questions per minute.

Rowe (1974a; 1974b) discovered that this pattern of rapid-fire questioning could be altered dramatically by having teachers increase their *wait time*. Wait time, which some teachers call thinking time, refers either to the interval between teacher question and student response, or to the interval between student response and subsequent teacher question. Rowe found that teachers' typical wait time is one second or less. She recommends 3 to 5 seconds as the optimal wait time.

Rowe (1986) recently reviewed the research that she and others conducted on wait time over the past decade. The following are some positive effects of increased wait time on learning that were found:

1. The length of student responses increases between 300 percent and 700 percent.

2. More inferences are supported by evidence and logical argument.

3. The incidence of speculative thinking and student-generated questions increases.

4. Failures to respond to questions decrease, and classroom discipline improves.

5. Student achievement on cognitively complex test items improves.

Why is wait time such a potent teaching technique? One reason may be that wait time changes the social control pattern in the classroom. Several researchers (Mishler 1975; Dillon 1982a) observed that rapid-fire questioning provides a way for the teacher to maintain control over students' social and verbal behavior. As teachers increase wait time, students feel more in control of their behavior. They may also feel that the teacher is more interested in their ideas than in testing their ability to remember facts.

Respond to Student Answers Positively and Constructively

Feedback is an effective instructional technique at all grade levels, for all subjects. It is important, too, in question-and-answer exchanges.

Some teachers respond to student answers simply by repeating the answer. Borg and his colleagues (1970) found that elementary teachers repeated student answers an average of 31 times in a 20-minute lesson. There is no evidence that this feedback technique promotes student learning. In fact, it may condition students not to listen to each other since they expect the teacher to repeat each answer for them.

A more effective technique is to acknowledge and build upon students' ideas. For example, suppose that a student responded to the teacher question, "What caused the fish in the lake to die?" by saying, "High water acidity." The teacher might acknowledge and build on this idea by saying, "Good. High acidity is harmful to fish and other marine organisms." Gage (1978) reviewed the research that has been done on this technique and concluded that it is promoting students' academic achievement.

Another effective technique is to praise the student's answer if it is of sufficient quality. Brophy (1981) reviewed the research on teacher praise and concluded that praise is effective but only if it is specific and credible. Frequent praise that is trivial or inappropriate is not effective. Brophy also concluded that teacher praise has more effect on the learning of low-SES and insecure students than on the learning of high-SES and secure students.

What should the teacher do if the student has given a weak, inaccurate, or "don't know" response to a question? Some teachers provide negative feedback or ignore the answer and call on another student to respond. Rosenshine (1986) concluded from his review of research that it is more effective for teachers to reexplain the information or skills about which the student is uncertain. Another option is to ask questions when a student gives a weak or "don't know" response. A probing question provides a hint or clue that is intended to assist the student in strengthening his or her initial response. Some researchers (Mangano and Benton 1984; Gage 1978) found that probing questions are effective, but other researchers (Gall et al. 1978; Wright and Nuthall 1970) found that they neither help nor hinder student learning. It may be that the effectiveness of probing questions depends upon the type of student being assisted.

DOES TRAINING IMPROVE TEACHERS' ABILITY
TO ASK QUESTIONS?

Some researchers have been interested in whether training can bring teachers' questioning behavior more in line with recommended practice. The results of their research have been mostly positive.

Minicourses were developed in the latter part of the 1960s to improve teachers' questioning skills. Research on the minicourses demonstrated that they are effective in improving teachers' use of a broad range of questioning skills (Borg et al. 1970), including percentage of higher-cognitive questions (Gall et al. 1970; Klinzing, Klinzing-Eurich, and Tisher 1985), and degree of correspondence between the cognitive level of teachers' questions and student responses (Klinzing et al. 1985).

In a series of research studies, Klinzing and Klinzing-Eurich (in press) demonstrated that training in questioning skills is most effective when it includes these elements: presentation of theory; discrimination of one questioning technique from another; presentation of teachers modeling each technique; and extended practice with feedback in microteaching settings. Clearly this training model is more extensive than the one-shot experiences provided in typical preservice and inservice programs.

The need for extensive training also has been found in research on increasing teachers' wait time during question-and-answer exchanges. Rowe (1986) reviewed this research and concluded, "So far, the procedure that gets the most people to achieve relatively stable criterion 3-second wait times in classroom settings takes longer than we would like, 6 to 12 hours. Moreover, it is a bit aversive because it involves transcribing 10-minute segments of tape recordings from three teach-reteach cycles using groups of four students" (p. 46). Perhaps further research will find ways to make the training process more efficient.

A recent trend in research has been to test the effectiveness of training teachers in total strategies involving questioning rather than in individual questioning techniques. For example, Good, Grouws, and Ebmeier developed a program that trains teachers in a strategy for mathematics instruction that involves question-and-answer exchanges at each phase of a lesson: daily review; development; seatwork; homework; and special review. Several studies (Good, Grouws, and Ebmeier 1983; Gall et al. 1985) found that their training program is effective in improving both teacher instruction and student academic achievement.

Simons (1984) and Morris (1986) developed a program for training teachers in a strategy for instruction in reading comprehension. The strategy, called PSRT (Prepare, Structure, Read, Think), involves having teachers ask questions to assess what students already know about a reading passage, to help them see how the text is organized, and to help them reflect on the text after reading it. Their research demonstrated that the training program brings about change in teachers' instructional methods and may also increase students' reading skills.

IS IT HELPFUL TO TRAIN STUDENTS IN QUESTION-ANSWERING AND QUESTION-GENERATING SKILLS?

Until a few years ago, most research on questioning focused on teachers. Now researchers have become interested in *students'* questioning skills. These skills are generally of two types: skills for answering the teachers' questions, and skills for generating their own questions.

Question-Answering Skills

Answering a question is a complex process. Singer (1986) stated, "The study of the cognition of question answering has yielded considerable agreement about its major stages ... question answering is thought to require the parsing and propositional encoding of the question, the identification of the question category, the retrieval of the requested information from short-term memory (STM) and/or long-term memory (LTM), and the output of the response" (p. 238). Because question answering is a complex process, educators should not assume that all students will learn it on their own.

Raphael and her colleagues conducted several studies (Raphael and Wonnacott 1985) to test the effectiveness of a procedure to improve elementary school students' ability to answer three types of comprehension questions: "Right There" questions, which can be answered directly from the text; "Think and Search" questions, which require the reader to make inferences using information in the text; and "On My Own" questions, which require an answer that comes from students' prior knowledge. The procedure involves teaching students the relationship between each type of question, the text to which it refers, and some knowledge the reader already has. Her research findings demonstrate that students can learn these relationships, with resulting improvement in their question-answering ability. Futhermore, regular teachers

39

can be trained to teach these procedures to their students.

The research of Raphael and her colleagues involves questions in classroom instruction. Students also answer questions on tests, and so researchers have investigated whether training improves students' ability to answer them. Davey and McBride (1986) reviewed this line of research and concluded that training programs are effective in improving students' ability to recognize and answer the different types of test questions.

Question-Generating Skills

The most exciting new area of research on questioning involves training students to generate their own questions as they study textbook material. The apparent advantage of this is that it encourages students to engage in active reading and to become aware of their own learning processes. In particular, question-generating helps students realize when they are comprehending or failing to comprehend the text. As stated above, this type of awareness is called *metacognition* by researchers.

Wong (1985) reviewed 27 studies of student question-generating and found positive effects on student reading comprehension in the majority of them. Studies that failed to find positive effects usually provided inadequate training for students in question-generating, and insufficient time for them to read and generate questions about the text.

One study (Garner and Alexander 1982) found that good readers, even without training, are likely to use question-generating as a strategy for comprehending text. An implication of this result is that training in question-generating may be more important for low-performing students than for high-performing students. In fact, Wong and Jones (1982) found that such training improved the achievement of learning-disabled students but not of normal students.

Several researchers have developed systematic programs of training for students in question-generating skills. One such program (Davey and McBride 1986) involves five sessions in which elementary school children are taught the distinction between literal and inferential questions and the criteria for determining important information in a reading passage. The training provides direct instruction, teacher modeling, and guided practice with feedback. Their research demonstrated that this training program is effective in improving students' reading comprehension.

A different approach to training question-generating skills was developed by Palincsar and Brown (1984). Their training program,

40

called *reciprocal teaching*, involves teaching students to generate questions about a section of text, to summarize it, to note or solicit points to be clarified, and to predict what will happen next. Each student in the reading group takes turns being the "teacher" by engaging in these four activities after each section of text. Training is done by means of explanation, modeling, practice, and corrective feedback with encouragement. Palincsar and Brown demonstrated that their training program is highly effective in improving the reading comprehension of low-performing junior high students.

CONCLUSION

Much is still not known about questions and how to use them to facilitate learning—particularly, the effects of questions on students' attitudes and feelings. Yet the research to date has produced several clear findings. Having reviewed these findings, we offer the following recommendations to teachers:

1. Ask questions frequently, but be careful not to ask them in such a way as to constrict students' thinking or to make them anxious. Also, be aware that extensive question-asking may become less necessary as students develop their own strategies for learning and reviewing.

2. Ask students questions before, during, and after instruction. Questions before instruction should be designed to get students to think about what they already know so that they can better assimilate new curriculum content. Questions during instruction should be used to keep students involved and provide a check on whether they are comprehending. And questions after instruction—in the form of seatwork, homework, review sessions, and practice quizzes—provide opportunities for continued practice and application of new information and skills.

3. During instruction, ask students questions about the facts, ideas, and thought processes that you think are particularly important. Students are likely to remember these facts, ideas, and processes better if you do so.

41

4. Ask lower-cognitive questions for your curriculum objectives at that level. Also, ask higher-cognitive questions if thinking skills are an objective of your curriculum. It is difficult to imagine how students will learn to think unless they have repeated opportunities to respond to higher-cognitive questions. Keep in mind that lower-performing students may have more difficulty dealing with these questions than will high-performing students.

5. Simply asking a good question—especially a good higher-cognitive question—does not guarantee a good student response. Therefore, use these techniques: provide controlled practice and remind students to listen in order to maintain a high level of on-task behavior; phrase questions clearly; pause at least 3 seconds after asking a question and after a student response; give positive feedback; and ask probing questions.

6. If you wish to improve your questioning skills, seek appropriate training experiences that are more than "one-shot" workshops. The training should include presentation of theory and models, extended practice, and personalized feedback.

7. Help your students develop good question-answering and question-generating skills. Training programs for these purposes are not generally available, so you will need to develop your own classroom activities for this purpose.

It is especially important to follow these recommended practices if you are responsible for teaching low-performing students. Some of the recommendations cannot be easily implemented. First, it takes more time to cover curriculum content using questions in the way that is recommended. Also, it takes additional time to work with students to improve their question-answering and question-generating skills. Since the curriculum is already crowded, this means that something has to go. Unfortunately, educators do not have a good process for determining the priority that should be given to depth versus breadth of content coverage.

The other problem involved in implementing these recommendations concerns the use of higher-cognitive questions in instruction. Various critics of American education (e.g., Goodlad 1983) have observed that the curriculum emphasizes basic skills rather than the development of thinking skills—including skills of problem solving, evaluation, creative production, and analysis. So long as this condition prevails, training alone will not be sufficient to increase teachers' use of higher-cognitive questions. A change in curriculum is also needed.

The authors wish to acknowledge Professor J.T. Dillon for his careful reading and criticism of a draft of this chapter.

REFERENCES

Andre, T. "Does Answering Higher Level Questions While Reading Facilitate Productive Learning?" *Review of Educational Research* 49 (1979): 280-318.

Aschner, M. "Asking Questions to Trigger Thinking." *NEA Journal* 50 (1961): 44-46.

Aschner, M; Gallagher, J.; Afsar, S.; Jenne, W.; and Faar, H. *A System for Classifying Thought Processes in the Context of Classroom Verbal Interaction.* Urbana: University of Illinois, 1965.

Berliner, D. C., and Fisher, C. W. *Perspectives on Instructional Time.* New York: Longman, 1985.

Bloom, B. S., et al., eds. *Taxonomy of Educational Objectives, Handbook I: Cognitive Domain.* New York: David McKay, 1956.

Blosser, P. E. "Review of Research: Teacher Questioning Behavior in Science Classrooms." Columbus, Ohio: EPIC Clearinghouse for Science, Mathematics, and Environmental Education, 1979. ERIC Document ED 184 818.

Boomer, G. "Oracy in Australian Schools (Or Doing What Comes Naturally)." Paper presented at the Conference on Developing Oral Communication Competence in Children, Armidale, Australia, 1979. ERIC Document ED 180 033.

Borg, W.R.; Kelley, M.L.; Langer, P.; and Gall, M. *The Minicourse: A Microteaching Approach to Teacher Education.* New York: Macmillan, 1970.

Brophy, J. "Teacher Praise: A Functional Analysis." *Review of Educational Research* 51 (1981): 5-32.

Davey, B., and McBride, S. "Effects of Question-Generation Training on Reading Comprehension." *Journal of Educational Psychology* 78 (1986): 256-62.

Dillon, J. T. "Cognitive Correspondence Between Question/Statement and

Response." *American Educational Research Journal* 19 (1982b); 540-51.

_____. "The Effect of Questions in Education and Other Enterprises." *Journal of Curriculum Studies* 14 (1982a): 127-52.

_____. "To Question and Not to Question During Discussion. II. Nonquestioning Techniques." *Journal of Teacher Education* 32 (November-December 1981a): 15-20.

_____. "To Question and Not to Question During Discussion. I. Questioning and Discussion." *Journal of Teacher Education* 32 (1981b): 51-55.

_____. "Questioning." In *A Handbook of Communication Skills*, edited by O. Hargie, pp. 95-127. London: Croom Helm, 1986.

_____. "Using Questions to Depress Student Thought." *School Review* 87 (1978): 50-63.

Dunkin, M.J., and Biddle, B.J. *The Study of Teaching*. New York: Holt, Rinehart & Winston, 1974.

Durkin, D. "What Classroom Observations Reveal About Reading Comprehension Instruction." *Reading Research Quarterly* 14 (1978-79): 481-533.

Eddinger, S. S. "The Effect of Different Question Sequences on Achievement in High School Social Studies." *Journal of Social Studies Research* 9 (1985): 17-29.

Frase, L. T. "Learning from Prose Material: Length of Passage, Knowledge of Results, and Position of Questions." *Journal of Educational Psychology* 58 (1967): 266-72.

Gage, N. L. *The Scientific Basis of the Art of Teaching*. New York: Teachers College Press, 1978.

Gall, M. D. "Discussion Methods of Teaching." In *The International Encyclopedia of Education*, edited by T. Husen and T. N. Postlethwaite. Oxford: Pergamon Press, 1985.

_____. "Synthesis of Research on Teachers' Questioning." *Educational Leadership* 2 (1984): 40-47.

_____. "The Use of Questions in Teaching." *Review of Educational Research* 40 (1970): 707-21.

Gall, M. D., and Gall, J. P. *Study for Success*. Eugene, Oreg.: M. Damien Publishers, 1985.

Gall, M. D., Fielding, G.; Schalock, D.; Charters, W. W., Jr., and Wilczinski, J. M. "Involving the Principal in Teachers' Staff Development: Effects on the Quality of Mathematics Instruction in Elementary School." Paper presented at the annual meeting of the American Educational Research Association, Chicago, April 1985.

Gall, M.D.; Gersten, R.; Erickson, D.; Grace, D.; and Stieber, S. "Instructional Correlates of Achievement Gains in Algebra Classes for High-Performing High School Students." Paper presented at the annual meeting of the American Educational Research Association, Washington, D.C., April 1987.

Gall, M.D.; Ward, B.A.; Berliner, D.C.; Cahen, L.S.; Winne, P.H.; Elashoff, J.D.; and Stanton, G.C. "Effects of Questioning Techniques and Recitation on Student Learning." *American Educational Research Journal* 15 (Spring 1978): 175-99.

Gall, M.D., et al. "Main Field Test Report: Minicourse 9—Thought Questions in the Intermediate Grades." Berkeley, Calif.: Far West Laboratory for Educational Research and Development, 1970.

Gambrell, L.B. "The Occurrence of Think-Time During Reading Comprehension." *Journal of Educational Research* 77 (1983): 77-80.

Garner, R., and Alexander, P. "Strategic Processing of Text: An Investigation of the Effects on Adults' Question-Answering Performance." *Journal of Educational Research* 75 (1982): 144-48.

Gersten, R.; Gall, M.; Grace, D.; Erickson, D.; and Stieber, S. "Instructional Correlates of Achievement Gains in Algebra Classes for Low-Performing High School Students." Paper presented at the annual meeting of the American Educational Research Association, Washington, D.C., April 1987.

Good, T.L.; Grouws, D.A.; and Ebmeier, H. *Active Mathematics Teaching*. New York: Longman, 1983.

Goodlad, J.I. *A Place Called School.* New York: McGraw-Hill, 1983.

Hamaker, C. "The Effects of Adjunct Questions on Prose Learning." *Review of Educational Research* 56 (1986): 212-42.

Hansen, J. "The Effects of Inference Training and Practice on Young Children's Comprehension." *Reading Research Quarterly* 16 (1981): 391-417.

Hansen, J., and Pearson, P.D. "An Instructional Study: Improving the Inferential Comprehension of Fourth Grade Good and Poor Readers." *Journal of Educational Psychology* 75 (1983): 821-29.

Hare, V.C., and Pulliam, C.A. "Teacher Questioning: A Verification and an Extension." *Journal of Reading Behavior* 12 (1980): 69-72.

Hargie, O.D. "The Importance of Teacher Questions in the Classroom." *Educational Research* 20 (1978): 99-102.

Hillman, S.B. "Information Processing as a Function of Question Type and Position." Paper presented at the annual meeting of the American Educational Research Association, San Francisco, 1979. ERIC Document ED 175 171.

Hoetker, J. "Teacher Questioning Behavior in Nine Junior High School English Classes." *Research in the Teaching of English* 2 (1968): 99-106.

45

Hoetker, W. J., and Ahlbrand, W. P. "The Persistence of the Recitation." *American Educational Research Journal* 6 (March 1969): 145-67.

Klinzing, H. G., and Klinzing-Eurich, G. "Research on Teacher Questioning in West Germany." *Questioning Exchange,* in press.

Klinzing, H. G.; Klinzing-Eurich, G.; and Tisher R.P. "Higher Cognitive Behaviors in Classroom Discourse: Congruencies Between Teachers' Questions and Pupils' Responses." *The Australian Journal of Education* 29 (1985): 63-75.

McKenzie, G. R. "Effects of Questions and Test-like Events on Achievement and On-Task Behavior in a Classroom Concept Learning Presentation." *Journal of Educational Research* 72 (1979): 348-51.

————. "Quizzes: Tools or Tyrants." *Instructional Science* 2 1973): 281-94.

McKenzie, G. R., and Henry, M. "Effects of Test-like Events on On-Task Behavior, Test Anxiety, and Achievement in a Classroom Rule-Learning Task." *Journal of Educational Psychology* 71 (1979): 370-74.

Mangano, N. G., and Benton, S. L. "Comparison of Question-Response Feedback Interactions During Basal Reader Instruction." *Journal of Educational Research* 78 (1984): 119-26.

Martin, J. "Effects of Teacher Higher-Order Questions on Student Process and Product Variables in a Single-Classroom Study." *Journal of Educational Research* 72 (1979): 183-87.

Mills, S. R.; Rice, C. T.; Berliner, D. C.; and Rousseau, E. W. "Correspondence Between Teacher Questions and Student Answers in Classroom Discourse." *Journal of Experimental Education* 48 (Spring 1980): 194-204.

Mishler, E. G., "Studies in Dialogue and Discourse II. Types of Discourse Initiated by and Sustained Through Questioning." *Journal of Psycholinguistic Research* 4 (1975): 99-121.

Morris, J. B. "The Effects of Training Teachers in a Schema-Based Comprehension Instruction Strategy on Teachers' Classroom Behavior and Students' Reading Achievement." Ph.D. diss., University of Oregon, 1986.

Palincsar, A. S., and Brown, A. L. "Reciprocal Teaching of Comprehension-Fostering and Monitoring Activities." *Cognition and Instruction* 1 (1984): 117-75.

Pearson, P. D., and Johnson, D. D. *Teaching Reading Comprehension*, New York: Holt, Rinehart and Winston, 1978.

Raphael, T. E., and Wonnacott, C. A. "Heightening Fourth-Grade Students' Sensitivity to Sources of Information for Answering Comprehension Questions." *Reading Research Quarterly* 20 (1985): 282-96.

Redfield, D. L., and Rousseau, E. W. "A Meta-Analysis of Experimental Research on Teacher Questioning Behavior." *Review of Educational Research* 51 (Summer 1981): 237-45.

Rosenshine, B. V. "Classroom Instruction." In *The Psychology of Teaching Methods*, edited by N. L. Gage. Chicago: University of Chicago Press, 1976.

————. "Synthesis of Research on Explicit Teaching." *Educational Leadership* 43 (April 1986): 60-69.

————. *Teaching Behaviors and Student Achievement*. London: National Foundation for Educational Research in England and Wales, 1971.

Rowe, D. W. "Does Research Support the Use of 'Purpose Questions' on Reading Comprehension Tests?" *Journal of Educational Measurement* 23 (1986): 43-55.

Rowe, M. B. "Relations of Wait Time and Rewards to the Development of Language, Logic and Fate Control: Part Two—Rewards." *Journal of Research in Science Teaching* 11 (1974): 291-308.

————. "Wait Time and Reward as Instructional Variables, Their Influence on Language, Logic, and Fate Control: Part One—Wait Time." *Journal of Research in Science Teaching* 11 (1974): 81-94.

————. "Wait Time: Slowing Down May Be a Way of Speeding Up!" *Journal of Teacher Education* (1986): 43-49.

Saxon, J. "Incremental Development: A Breakthrough in Mathematics." *Phi Delta Kappan* 63 (1982): 482-84.

Seretny, M. L., and Dean, R. S. "Interspersed Postpassage Questions and Reading Comprehension Achievement." *Journal of Educational Psychology* 78 (1986): 228-29.

Simons, S. M. "The Effects of Training Secondary Teachers in a Reading Comprehension Instruction Strategy Based on Schema Theory." Ph.D., diss., University of Oregon, 1984.

Singer, M. "Answering Wh- Questions About Sentences and Text." *Journal of Memory and Language* 25 (1986): 238-54.

Sirotnik, K. "What You See Is What You Get—Consistency, Persistency, and Mediocrity in the Classroom." *Harvard Educational Review* 53 (February 1983): 16-31.

Smith, C. W. "Verbal Behavior and Classroom Practice." Paper presented at the International Conference on Thinking, Cambridge, Mass., August 1984. ERIC Document ED 260 077.

Stevens, R. *The Question as a Means of Efficiency in Instruction: A Critical Study of Classroom Practice*. New York: Teachers College Press, 1912.

Walberg, H. J.; Paschal, R. A.; and Weinstein, T. "Homework: Powerful Effects on Learning." *Educational Leadership* 42 (April 1985): 76-79.

Wilson, M. M. "Processing Strategies of Average and Below Average Readers Answering Factual and Inferential Questions on Three Equivalent Passages." *Journal of Reading Behavior* 11 (Fall 1979): 234-45.

Winne, P. H. "Experiments Relating Teachers' Use of Higher Cognitive Questions to Student Achievement." *Review of Educational Research* 49 (Winter 1979): 13-49.

Wittrock, M. C. "Reading Comprehension." In *Neuropsychological and Cognitive Processes in Reading*, edited by F. J. Pirozzolo and M. C. Wittrock. New York: Academic Press, 1981.

Wixson, K. K. "Questions About a Text: What You Ask About Is What Children Learn." *The Reading Teacher* (December 1983): 287-93.

Wong, B. Y. L. "Increasing Retention of Main Ideas Through Questioning Strategies." *Learning Disabilities Quarterly* 2 (1979): 42-47.

_____. "Self-Questioning Instructional Research: A Review." *Review of Educational Research* 55 (1985): 227-68.

Wong, B. Y. L., and Jones, W. "Increasing Meta-Comprehension in Learning Disabled and Normally Achieving Students Through Self-Questioning Training." *Learning Disabilities Quarterly* 5 (1982): 228-39.

Wright, C. J., and Nuthall, G. "Relationships Between Teacher Behaviors and Pupil Achievement in Three Elementary Science Lessons." *American Educational Research Journal* 7 (1970): 477-93.

3. THE MULTIDISCIPLINARY WORLD OF QUESTIONING

by J. T. Dillon, Associate Professor of Education, University of California, Riverside

Consultant: Todd D. Kelley, Shoreham-Wading River Central School District, Shoreham, New York

What in the world do other people know and do about questioning? A tour beyond the school shows how questions are used and understood in a dozen realms of practice and a dozen realms of theory. Instead of a few novel techniques, the lesson brought home to education is the notion that questions are used to serve purpose in circumstance. A theoretical understanding of questions and answers is the best practical guide to using them for purposes of classroom teaching and learning.

In the world outside school there lie multiple domains of questioning. We will take a tour of this world in just the way we might take a packaged tour of Europe, seeing seven countries in four days. Frazzled but vaguely exhilarated, we come home knowing at least that the countries are there, and we remember scattered sights of interest that we plan to revisit someday for a closer look.

As a device for our tour, we will divide the world into realms of question-answer *practice* and question-answer *theory*, visiting a dozen fields in each realm but making only one stop per field and seeing only one or two sights per stop. Recent books will be our guide: one or two books per field, a point or two per book. As a result, we will not know much about the book, far less about the field, but we will have learned some interesting pointers for understanding and practice of questioning. We will see nothing of education, since that is the field we are leaving

49

behind in the first place in order to see what else is out there in the world of questioning. At the end we will see what lessons we bring home for teaching and learning.

We begin with what most of us are interested in seeing, points of practice. But the most interesting sights and useful points will come later, in realms of theory.

REALMS OF PRACTICE

In some fields beyond the school, practice consists almost entirely of asking questions. In other fields, questions are essential to practice. People who design questionnaires and conduct interrogations, for example, are by definition asking questions.

Surveys and Opinion Polls

Asking Questions (Sudman and Bradburn 1982) is a practical guide to questionnaire design for practitioners in various fields who regularly approach people and ask them questions in order to find out their true opinion, preferences, habits, and attitudes about anything. The overall problem is to ask questions that will get reliable answers. Respondents agreeably give all manner of distorted answers to most kinds of questions, especially to those that are felt to have a right/wrong answer. These are "threatening" questions and they concern such things as whether the respondent holds a library card or agrees with the statement in question. Therefore, one of the many things that the questioner must do is to ask threatening questions in a nonthreatening way, and to appear and to be nonjudgmental.

Above all the questioner must word the question in such a way that everyone will understand it, and understand it just as it is intended. That turns out to be difficult, at least for the experts in this field. For example, "What brand of soft drink do you usually buy?" looks clear and specific enough until you ask it of people. Respondents range all over as they decide what time period "usually" involves, which conditions or settings apply for "buy," who is included in "you," and what counts as a "soft drink" (p. 39).

Most questioners believe that asking questions is a simple matter that does not require great skill, judgment, experience, or even much time or effort to prepare. The experts know better than that. They advise writing the questions out and then testing and revising them no less than four times before going on to ask them, otherwise *don't ask the questions* (p. 283).

The experts who conducted the 200 experiments in *Questions and Answers in Attitude Surveys* (Schuman and Presser 1981) despair of their ability to construct questions immune from serious criticism and they remain uncertain about the effects of questions (pp. 13, 77). However, they know some interesting things about what questions do.

For example, people tend to choose the last-listed of two to three alternatives, whatever it says. Divorce should be made harder to obtain if "harder" is listed last; easier to get if "easier" is last; and stay as is if "as is" is last. People also choose specific answers to closed questions that they would never supply in answer to open questions. They select "to think for themselves" as the most important thing for chidren to learn in life but hardly mention it at all when asked what the most important thing is for children to learn in life. More people will agree with the other side of the argument when some consideration is added in support of it. "Some people think yes because of this and other people think no because of that; yes or no?" Otherwise people just agree with the interviewer and say yes. Finally, more people will say "I don't know" when permitted to answer "I don't know" and more will correct a mistaken question when permitted to correct a mistaken question. Otherwise most people agreeably answer yes and let it go at that.

In all of these ways, people readily answer by telling the questioner what they don't think while the questioner pushes on with more questions to find out what people think.

Investigation and Interrogation

Police, private detectives, and insurance examiners ask questions of all manner of people in order to get truthful, factual information from them about some civil or criminal matter. The way they use questions is familiar to us from novels, TV, movies, and other fantastic depictions. *Interviews and Interrogations* (Buckwalter 1983) tells us instead how practicing investigators do it. They ask questions in interviews with cooperative informants and in interrogations with reluctant ones, innocent as well as guilty people who conceal or otherwise withhold information for several good reasons.

51

The informant has the information; the investigator wants it. The questioning has to be such as to obtain all that information and to avoid inhibiting its full disclosure. For example, the interrogator avoids rapid-fire questions and trick questions, instead asking straightforward questions slowly enough to give the informant all the time he/she wishes for a complete answer and then to qualify the answer as he/she will. The interrogator asks questions in a conversational tone and in a winsome manner, showing himself/herself to be genuine, truthful, trustworthy, concerned, courteous, nonjudgmental, sympathetic, and understanding—as well as patient and persistent in the questioning (p. 78). Another book, *The Gentle Art of Interviewing and Interrogation* (Royal and Schutt 1976), is a guide on how to ask people questions if you want to find out what they know.

If survey-takers hear lies from people about drinking soda pop, borrowing library books, and donating to charity, interrogators have to hear the truth from people implicated in rapine and mayhem, thievery and butchery, among other more fraughtful matters. Naturally, the interrogator carefully avoids using precise words, asking instead about having sex with the girl, doing it, taking the thing, and cutting the man. And they listen most carefully to the answers.

Questioning and listening is the basic practice in interrogation (Buckwalter 1983, p. 37). Interrogators take care to prepare the questions that they are going to ask, planning them and writing them down beforehand. Of course, only the most experienced interrogators need to do that, and only the best ones have to listen to the answers. (All interrogators are well advised to do so.) Today's local newspaper headlines: "Detective Solves Old Murder Case by Listening." The unsuspected murderer, who was actually in jail at the (mistakenly established) time of death, liked to chat with this detective during his frequent arrests for trifling matters, because this detective listened to him. The scene of the interrogation that broke the case was the neighborhood grocery store where they often met while shopping. "He just liked talking to me, I guess," ventured the hero. "I didn't treat him like dirt." So much for tricks of interrogation.

Scientific Interrogation (Taylor 1984) supplies the gumshoe with a technical panoply of hypnosis, polygraphy, narcoanalysis, voice stress analysis, and pupillometrics. But the questioning remains the same as without these scientific techniques. The interrogator is now even more careful to avoid suggestive questions and rapid questioning, giving plenty of time for answers and even rehearsing the questions with the informant beforehand to make sure that there are no surprises and no mistakes over words. As before, innocent as well as guilty informants feel threatened by the questions and will lie, even in response to the "noncrime" questions. "Prior to this year, did you ever want to see anyone seriously hurt?" And as before, the worth of the answers depends on the skill of the questioner, no matter the science of the technique: the informants can't beat the machine but they can beat the interrogator (p. 286).

Courtroom Examination

Lawyers rely on questioning to get information favorable to their case stated by a witness who is coerced to answer the questions as asked. *Questioning Techniques and Tactics* (Kestler 1982) advises them on how to ask questions of witnesses who do not want to give the information.

For example, during cross-examination the questions are to be fast-paced, keeping the witness off-balance and ramming home his or her subordinate status, giving him or her no time to think or to formulate the answer carefully (pp. 46-47). The examiner is never to ask "Why?" or to use questions with alternatives but only to ask yes/no questions to which he or she already knows the answer. Dramatic depictions have taught us how facile and ready the questioning is, astonishing as that must be in light of the 33 principles and 44 techniques that lawyers are told to use, and all the more remarkable in light of the observed "Strategic Use of Questions in Court" (Woodbury 1984), where lawyers are seen to ask systematically different questions when prosecuting and defending, with friendly and hostile, naive and expert witnesses, during direct and cross-examination, in trial and pretrial proceedings, and courtroom and extra-courtroom contexts.

The experts seem to find it difficult to ask questions rightly. They think it imperative to interview all witnesses before deposing or examining them (Kestler 1982, p. 104), and to write down the questions, arranging them in logical sequence, before asking them aloud. The questions are then asked in a hop-skip-and-jump approach that eliminates any semblance of orderly progression (p. 123). That is no trick; the trick is not to confuse yourself and the jury. Lastly, the lawyer takes care to listen to the answers (p. 147). Sharp, young lawyers, of course, can spend the answer time thinking up a crafty question to ask next, since they know how to think on their feet; the old hands have to spend all kinds of time writing out the questions beforehand and then they have to stand there and listen to the answers. (The young hands are well advised to follow their lead.)

Witnesses are also told how to answer questions. Friendly witnesses are rehearsed before the questioning begins, and they are coached to speak only if, when, and as asked, to supply no more information than called for, and not to state their opinion (e.g., p. 34). They are warned that being questioned is a physical and emotional ordeal (p. 339).

Counseling and Psychotherapy

Counselors, therapists, and psychiatrists are often seen to ask many questions of an insightful and revealing character, especially when the therapeutic session has to be accomplished dramatically in a few moments on the screen. *Questioning* (Long, Paradise, and Long 1981) reveals the difficulty that experienced therapists have in using questions appropriately, and differently, at each of the successful stages of the process; and it cautions against the inappropriate use of questions with harmful consequences while encouraging the facilitative use of questions with helpful consequences.

"Questions and Counseling" (Baldwin 1987) reveals the perplexities of practice in a field where certain guides forbid the therapist from asking any questions at all on grounds of foiling the process, while others direct the therapist only to ask questions on grounds of facilitating the process. "The Use of Questioning as a Psychoanalytic Technique" (Olinick 1954) warns analysts, darkly as usual, that their questions may serve only their own unconscious needs and unresolved anxieties in an effort to dominate and master the patient in a nontherapeutic pregenital relationship, while specifying that in some cases the deviant technical intervention of a question can be resorted to as therapeutically valid if the patient neither welcomes nor resists the questioning.

This series of contrasts describes not so much different practices as different purposes being served in different contexts and perhaps even different fields of practice.

Journalism

Creative Interviewing (Metzler 1977) guides print and broadcast journalists in asking questions to get information or colorful remarks from people. The basis is supposed to be curiosity, and the sequence of questions follows "the rambling dictates of natural curiosity" (p. 67). But the questions are to be thoroughly prepared beforehand, in nine different categories, each with several types. For example, eight types of probe questions are available for use with the famous princess who, when asked if lack of interest in men was the reason she never married, answers: "Young man, I've had 33 lovers in 20 years!"—Who do you have in mind for No. 34? runs one probe.

For learning how to ask questions, the journalist does well to answer questions from an unskilled and inexperienced interviewer (p. 139).

Library Reference

Informational Interviews and Questions (Slavens 1978) trains reference librarians to negotiate the question that a patron asks before they go on to answer it. For example, a man wants to order a book for his wife but can't remember the author or title.

> Do you remember what the book is about?
> —It's an art book.
> Do you know if it was about the art of a certain period or country?
> —It could be about Mexican art and it costs $30. (p. 72)

Another man has heard something on the radio about the largest check ever written but is not sure.

> Anyway, could you find out some more information about it for me?
> —How much information do you need?
> Oh, I'd like to know how much it was for and what bank it was drawn on and who it was paid to. (p. 111)

On the other hand, a schoolboy asks,

> Where can I find a critical essay on "The Duty of Civil Disobedience"?
> —Who wrote it?
> It doesn't matter. I just need an essay. (p. 53)

In most cases studied (Lynch 1978), the librarian discovers that the patron's initial question is not the question he or she is asking. Although librarians are urged to use open questions with the patron, 90 percent of their questions are closed. "Do you mean train conductors or orchestra conductors?" Maybe electrical conduits.

It seems a blunder to answer a person's question before you and he or she are sure of the question that is being asked.

Other Fields

Questions in Parliament (Chester and Bowring 1962) shows how members ask questions and ministers answer them—hundreds a day, 40,000 per session. *Questioning Techniques* (Kaiser 1979) is a practical guide to asking questions in everyday situations and in various contexts such as personnel interviews, oral examinations, and sales conversations. (Still other fields practice questioning but their practices figure in journal articles rather than books.)

What to Study (Campbell, Daft, and Hulin 1982) guides scholarly researchers in raising questions about the world, and *Questions Are the Answer* (Robinson 1980) guides religious believers in raising questions about the other world, so to speak.

Questions Children Ask (Hughes 1981) shows children asking questions about matters big and little—death, God, sex, and "Where does your lap go when you stand up?"—and it advises parents on how to answer them. There is no book called *Questions Pupils Ask* since children do not ask enough questions in school to fill a book.

REALMS OF THEORY

In the world beyond education, which is not a discipline and has no theory of questioning, lie a dozen disciplines of study where question-answer theories or models are constructed. Questions are not the defining topic of these disciplines, nor is making models of question-answer theories their essential business—except in two cases. The last of these to be surveyed is philosophy, where the business is to question; and the first is erotetic logic, a new field that defines itself by the analysis of question-answer.

Logic

The Logic of Questions and Answers (Belnap and Steel 1976) is concerned with precise formal analysis of concepts, types, and relations of "questions," "answer," and associated terms such as presupposition and raise. A question arises, and can be answered, just in case its presupposition is true. For example—logicians for some reason use formal language and funny examples—"Is the present king of France bald?" is a favorite false question, presupposing that there is a present king of France and that he is either bald or not bald. (cf., "Have you stopped beating your wife?")

Dumb questions have no direct answer, and safe answers repeat the question's presupposition.

> Was it suicide or murder?
> Well, it was one or the other.

A complete answer to "When is glass a liquid?" is "Glass is a liquid at 70° F, and China is populous." (A *just*-complete answer would drop the needless point about China.) A partial answer (implied by a direct answer) to "Was her ladyship wearing the green dress, the emerald bracelet, or both?" is "She was wearing green," whereas "She was naked" is a corrective answer, implying the denial of every direct answer by rejecting the truth of the question's presupposition. A key to understanding what questions are is to understand what answers are.

Information Science

Natural Language Question Answering Systems (Bolc 1980) shows how question and answer relate both theoretically and practically. For example, when busy officials monitoring industrial pollution unwittingly put dumb questions to the information system, the system corrects the questioner's false presuppositions and mistaken presumptions, supplying helpful information instead of the correct and direct but meaningless and misleading answer.

> What toxic elements were found in the November sample at VW?
> There was no November sample (versus "No toxic elements").
> How much should the fine be on the cyanide pollution in Stuttgart?
> Cadmium was found, not cyanide (versus "Sock 'em a million dollars a day!").

In other contexts, witnesses who "stonewall" give perfectly direct and correct answers to erroneous questions. The questioner has to ask endless little questions pointed this way and that, each yielding one more tiny bit of information, until it dawns that the original question was mistaken to begin with. "All right, so no minority candidates passed your department's test in November because you didn't even give any test in November. All right. Now how about December?"

Psychology and Artificial Intelligence

Together these form part of a new "cognitive science" discipline. *The Psychology of Questions* (Graesser and Black 1985) and *The Process of Question Answering* (Lehnert 1978), which gives a computer simulation of cognition, work out flow charts and models to represent how people comprehend and answer questions, especially written questions about textual material just read (a simple story or paragraph).

Although other branches of psychology also study questioning, the studies appear in journal articles rather than in books devoted to questioning.

Sociolinguistics

Questioning Strategies in Sociolinguistics (Churchill 1978) analyzes responding strategies in everyday conversations. People respond to questions with nonanswers of all kinds, all of them accepted, or at least tolerated by the questioner as long as what follows the question is recognizable as a response or, failing that, as long as the noncompliance can be explained away.

Questions and Responses in English Conversation (Stenstroem 1984) minutely analyzes the types and functions of question, response, plus followup reaction of the questioner. To yes/no questions people answer yes and stop; when they answer no they go on to elaborate and qualify, justifying their negative answer. The followup is optional in everyday conversation but obligatory in classrooms; and in classrooms, it evaluates the quality of the answer ("good answer") rather than reacting to the content of the message ("good news")—except in the rare case of student questions, where the followup is optional and never evaluative ("oh" or "thank you" but not "good!").

In general, the least thing that people do in reply to a question is to give an answer. Questioners need to know what the respondent is doing, and just when the question is being answered.

Linguistics

Interrogativity (Chisholm 1984) tells everything known about the syntax, semantics, and pragmatics of questioning in seven disparate languages, excluding English, but not surprisingly including Ute and

West Greenlandic. Russian bureaucrats and salespeople do not smile when asking *"What* do you want?" nor does the passerby who of a sudden puts his face in front of yours to ask, "Don't you *know* where Fourth Street is?" (p. 29)—two hostile and direct questions that are asked neutrally and politely in Russian, whereas the English way of asking them strikes Russians as excessive and hypocritical. (How are you this morning? Is there something that I might help you with today? Excuse me. I really hate to bother you, but would you by any chance happen to know where Fourth Street is?)

As for English, *Questions and Answers in English* (Pope 1976) gives a transformational-grammar analysis showing, for example, that rhetorical questions require a direct answer (p. 44). The answer is identical with the question's presupposition. Negative questions ("Isn't?") require positive answers, and positive questions ("Is"), negative answers. Yes disagrees with a positive question and no agrees with a negative one; to agree, say "Yea" and to disagree say "Nay" as of old (p. 111).

Discourse Analysis

Questions that are rhetorical, loaded, and anything else figure in *Dialogue Games* (Carlson, 1983), a game-theoretic analysis of the rules in a formal game with two rational players and two admissible moves, questions and answers, with the aim of arriving at a common understanding of the topic of the dialogue. Questions are construed to begin with "Bring it about that I know _____." So "Charles Dodgson" is not a satisfying answer to "Who wrote *Alice in Wonderland?*" when the questioner does not know either who Dodgson is, or Lewis Carroll. That analysis of questions comes originally from *The Semantics of Questions* (Hintikka 1976), where most of the examples, like those in *Dialogue Games*, come from detective novels or whodunits.

Philosophy of Science

Philosophers, logicians, historians, and methodologists of science display their question-answer models under a title that alone gives the basic theory, *Scientific Method as a Problem-Solving and Question-Answering Technique* (Hintikka 1981). "Questioning in Science" (Dillon 1987) reviews theory, research, and practice bearing on science as a question-answer process.

Hermeneutics and Literary Criticism

Literature is a process of asking and answering questions on the part of both author and reader. *Meaning and Reading* (Meyer 1983) shows that in producing a text, authors (figuratively) answer a question; in understanding the text, exegetes and critics (explicitly) construe the question to which the text is an answer. For the text as a whole and for individual sentences they ask: What question does this text answer? What qualifies it as an answer? They find the meaning of the text by finding the questions to which it answers as a text and by questioning its character as answer (p. 157). Literature thus safely opens questions that political ideology closes down or that other sensibilities forbid addressing. Reader and author join in the question-answer, each of them questioning and each answering. Understanding what you read is thus a matter of knowing not the statement that the text makes but the question-answer proposition that it forms to your sense.

Philosophy

The Need to Question (Clark 1973) is an introductory textbook whose title alone tells what philosophy is. *Perplexity and Knowledge* (Clark 1972) is an existential-transcendental analysis of the structures of questioning, showing what it is for the self to be a questioner and knower. "I need to question in order to know." Our knowledge, then, as one of the premier philosophers anciently proposed, consists in answers to questions (Aristotle, *Analytica Posteriora* 89b). Whose question? is a vital issue for determining knowledge.

Other Fields

Questions and Politeness (Goody 1978) proposes a theory of questioning from anthropology, based on observations of Gonja society. Other question-answer theories are found in various branches of disciplines other than those mentioned here (e.g., branches of psychology other than the cognitive or cognitive-science).

A variety of theories appear in interdisciplinary collections such as *Questions* (Hiz 1978), *Questions and Answers* (Kiefer 1983), and *Questions and Questioning* (Meyer, 1987).

Most of the variety of theory and the variety of practice from most fields and from most countries appear in the new journal, *Questioning Exchange: A Multidisciplinary Review* (published by Taylor and Francis of London).

LESSONS FOR TEACHING AND LEARNING

Instead of a bag of new tricks, the tired lesson brought home to education from this tour of the world of questioning is a singular notion that *questions are used to serve purpose in circumstance*. Which use of questions will serve pedagogical purposes in classroom circumstances? The answer is found in practice informed by theory.

A theoretical understanding of questions, and especially of answers, is the most practical guide to using questions in teaching. The first mandate is to know the elements of questioning so as to manipulate them according to purpose in circumstance (for details see Dillon 1986).

It is senseless for a teacher to use techniques that serve other purposes and circumstances. Moreover, educational purposes and circumstances vary, even within the same classroom. That makes it pointless to use a given technique and useless to point to specific techniques for practice. Better to understand what questions and answers are so as to bend them to this specific pedagogical purpose in this specific classroom circumstance—students and subject matter, level and activity, lessons past and aims projected. No specifiable types of questions or questioning behaviors can serve through this range of classroom practice, no more than any can serve across the diverse fields of question-answer practices.

Some good if general advice is nonetheless available to guide the practice of questioning in the broad classroom processes of recitation and discussion. Most of the multiple purposes within these will be well served by disciplining pedagogical behavior to prepare the questions beforehand, to ask them nicely and slowly, and to listen to the answers.

For example, as noted in our survey, skillful interrogators plan out and write down their questions beforehand; they avoid rapid-fire questioning and give plenty of time before and after the answer; and then they listen to the answers (Buckwalter 1983; Taylor 1984). Skilled cross-examiners too write out and arrange their questions beforehand and listen carefully to the answers (Kestler 1982). Journalists and opinion pollsters thoroughly prepare their questions—to the point of trying them out and revising them several times before actually asking them (Metzler 1977; Sudman and Bradburn 1982). As for teachers, these three general points are treated in great detail in a manual on questioning (Dillon 1987b). Here the points can only be noted as general lessons from our tour of the world of questioning.

1. *Prepare the questions*. Before asking questions, think about the

purpose for asking and plan the questions to be asked. Preparation includes the sorry labor of writing down the questions and reformulating them until they seem right, then tiresomely trying out the questions (e.g., with friends) to see if other people understand them as asked and answer them as anticipated. Only then are the questions ready for the asking.

2. *Go slowly.* While asking questions, keep the purpose for asking in mind and discipline your questioning behavior—tone, attitude, pace—according to that purpose in the present circumstance. Little educative purpose in any circumstance is served by asking questions at a fast pace, even during a recitation. It is better to have a gentle and leisurely exchange that allows, for but one example, students to formulate and to express what they are thinking or to recall and reveal what they know.

3. *Listen to the answers.* After asking, discipline yourself to attend to what the student is saying and doing in response. See how the purpose for asking is now being served. At the very least, look to see if what follows the question is an answer to it, and appreciate what the answer reveals about this student's state of mind.

Only the more skilled and experienced questioners actually need to prepare the questions beforehand, ask them nicely and slowly, and listen to the answers. (Inexperienced questioners too are well advised to do so.) As for the next step, it follows as a matter of course again to do something to purpose—for example, to ask another question. On that point teachers need no further advice. But they might welcome the intelligence that many nonquestioning alternatives are available as promising choices for interaction, especially during a discussion.

At the juncture where a student has just answered a question the teacher may, instead of asking a further question, choose one of an array of alternatives grouped into four classes. These give promise of enhancing the students' cognitive, affective, and expressive processes, fostering discussion (for details, see articles by Dillon 1979, 1981, 1984, 1985, or a book-length treatment in Dillon 1987b). Some of the nonquestioning alternatives are the following:

1. *Statements.* State the thought that occurs to you in relation to what the student has just said. Various kinds of statements may be made, such as a declarative statement of your thinking on the

matter in question or a reflective restatement of (your understanding of) the student's thought. The student will respond with further expression of more complex thought.

2. *Student Questions.* Provide that a student can ask a question related to what the speaker has just said. For instance, the speaker might formulate the question that is troubling him or her as he or she struggles to think and to express his or her thinking. In a recitation, students too might prepare and ask questions of one another, reciting their knowledge and understanding in an exchange of question-answer propositions that they have formed of the subject matter studied. Student response to student questions is longer and more complex than to teacher questions.

3. *Signals.* Indicate attentive reception of what the student has said, without yourself holding the floor. For instance, speakers are encouraged to go on by various fillers ("um-hm") and phatics ("Oh, how nice!").

4. *Silences.* Say nothing at all but maintain a deliberate, appreciative silence until the speaker resumes or another student enters in. To be noticeable the silence has to last an eternity, which in a classroom means three seconds or so. That is the time it takes to sing in your mind the protracted beginning of the anthem, "O-oh say, can you s-eeee?" or to chant "Baa baa black sheep, have you any wool?" while seeing if the student has any more to offer. If you hold out for the full three seconds, the student will hand over three bags full.

Or yet, alternatively, the teacher can choose to ask another question, preferably one that *perplexes self* about the matter in question, something grand or minor that self needs and wants to know and to understand. During a discussion especially, a perplexed question may well be the alternative of choice, whether asked by teacher or student.

Perplexed questions, as we have learned from our tour, are not the norm in the world of questioning. And we have learned from experience that they are not the norm in classrooms, either. Yet theory teaches us that these are the questions that stimulate thought and eventuate in knowledge. On those very grounds of theory, practice in education should stand out against other realms for its normally perplexed questioning in the service of learning.

REFERENCES

Baldwin, C. "Questions and Counseling." *Questioning Exchange* 1 (1987): 5-9.

Belnap, N. D., and Steel, T. B. *The Logic of Questions and Answers*. New Haven, Conn.: Yale University Press, 1976.

Bolc, L., ed. *Natural Language Question Answering Systems*. Munich: Hanser, 1980.

Buckwalter, A. *Interviews and Interrogations*. Stoneham, Mass.: Butterworth, 1983.

Campbell, J. P.; Daft, R. I..; and Hulin, C. L. *What to Study: Generating and Developing Research Questions*. Beverly Hills, Calif.: Sage, 1982.

Carlson, L. *Dialogue Games: An Approach to Discourse Analysis*. Dordrecht, Holland: Reidel, 1983.

Chester, D., and Bowring, N. *Questions in Parliament*. Oxford: Clarendon, 1962.

Chisholm, W., ed. *Interrogativity*. Amsterdam: Benjamins, 1984.

Churchill, L. *Questioning Strategies in Sociolinguistics*. Rowley, Mass.: Newbury, 1978.

Clark, M. *The Need to Question: An Introduction to Philosophy*. Englewood Cliffs, N.J.: Prentice-Hall, 1973.

_____. *Perplexity and Knowledge: An Inquiry into the Structures of Questioning*. The Hague: Nijhoff, 1972.

Dillon, J. T. "Alternatives to Questioning." *High School Journal* 62 (1979): 217-22.

_____. "To Question and Not to Question During Discussion II: Non-questioning Techniques." *Journal of Teacher Education* 32, no. 6 (1981): 15-20.

_____. "Research on Questioning and Discussion." *Educational Leadership* 42, no. 3 (1984): 50-56.

_____. "Using Questions to Foil Discussion." *Teaching and Teacher Education* 1 (1985): 109-121.

_____. "Questioning." In *A Handbook of Communications Skills*, edited by O. Hargie, Chap. 4, pp. 95-127. London: Croom Helm, 1986.

_____. "Questioning in Science." In *Questions and Questioning: An Interdisciplinary Reader*, edited by M. Meyer. Berlin: De Gruyter, 1987.

_____. *Questioning and Teaching: A Manual of Practice*. London: Croom

Helm, and New York: Methuen, 1987b.

Goody, E. N., ed. *Questions and Politeness: Strategies in Social Interaction.* Cambridge: Cambridge University Press, 1978.

Graesser, A., and Black, J., eds. *The Psychology of Questions.* Hillsdale, N.J.: Erlbaum, 1985.

Hintikka, J., ed. *Scientific Method as a Problem-Solving and Question-Answering Technique.* Dordrecht, Holland: Reidel, 1981 (special issue of *Synthese* 47, whole no. 1).

_____. *The Semantics of Questions.* Amsterdam: North-Holland, 1976.

Hiz, H., ed. *Questions.* Dordrecht, Holland: Reidel, 1978.

Hughes, J. *Questions Children Ask.* Tring, England: Lion, 1981.

Kaiser, A. *Questioning Techniques.* Pomona, Calif.: Hunter, 1979.

Kestler, J. L. *Questioning Techniques and Tactics.* Colorado Springs, Colo.: Shepard/McGraw-Hill, 1982.

Kiefer. F., ed. *Questions and Answers.* Dordrecht, Holland: Reidel, 1983.

Lehnert, W. G. *The Process of Question Answering: A Computer Simulation of Cognition.* Hillsdale, N.J.: Erlbaum, 1978.

Long, L.; Paradise, L.; and Long., T. *Questioning: Skills for the Helping Process.* Monterey, Calif.: Brooks/Cole, 1981.

Lynch, M. J. "Reference Interviews in Public Libraries." *Library Quarterly* 48 (1978): 119-42.

Metzler, K. *Creative Interviewing: The Writer's Guide to Gathering Information by Asking Questions.* Englewood Cliffs, N.J.: Prentice-Hall, 1977.

Meyer, M. *Meaning and Reading.* Amsterdam: Benjamins, 1983.

_____, ed. *Questions and Questioning: An Interdisciplinary Reader.* Berlin: De Gruyter, 1987.

Olinick, S. L. "Some Considerations of the Use of Questioning as a Psychoanalytic Technique. *Journal of the American Psychoanalytic Association* 2 (1954): 57-66.

Pope, E. *Questions and Answers in English.* The Hague: Mouton, 1976.

Robinson, W. *Questions Are the Answer: Believing Today.* New York: Pilgrim Press, 1980.

Royal, R. F., and Schutt, S. *The Gentle Art of Interviewing and Interrogation.* Englewood Cliffs, N.J.: Prentice-Hall, 1976.

Schuman, H., and Presser, S. *Questions and Answers in Attitude Surveys.* New York: Academic Press, 1981.

Slavens, T.P., ed. *Informational Interviews and Questions*. Metuchen, N.J.: Scarecrow Press, 1978.

Stenstroem, A. B. *Questions and Responses in English Conversation*. Malmo, Sweden: Gleerup, 1984.

Sudman, S., and Bradburn, N. M. *Asking Questions*. San Francisco: Jossey-Bass, 1982.

Taylor, L. *Scientific Interrogation*. Charlottesville, Va.: Michie, 1984.

Woodbury, H. "The Strategic Use of Questions in Court." *Semiotica* 48 (1984): 197-228.

4. WHAT KIND OF QUESTION IS THAT?

by Roger T. Cunningham, Professor of Education, The Ohio State University, Columbus

Consultants: Bettye Myer, Assistant Professor of Education, Miami University, Ohio; and Larry Wills, Assistant Dean, College of Education and Allied Professions, Bowling Green State University, Ohio

The characteristics, purposes, and values of different kinds of questions from the cognitive and affective domains are explored. Relationships between questions from the two domains are highlighted to show how teachers can use both kinds of questions during classroom discussions. Several examples of different kinds of questions are provided so that the reader has numerous models for developing his/her own questions. Finally, an illustration of how to coordinate questions from the two domains is given.

What kinds of questions do you ask? Have you thought about it? Do you think it is important enough to contemplate? What have you done about it? Are you satisfied with the answers you get to your questions? You were just asked a number of questions. Each question asks for a very different response. Each question probably caused you to think in a different way. Did you recognize the differences? Like some things in life, the differences can be subtle; like other things in life, a little bit of difference is terribly important. Hooray, for the "little bit of difference"! How you ask and present questions can make a difference to your students and can have a positive impact on student learning. One of the most useful tools available to you is the right kinds of questions.

The purpose of this chapter is to make you more aware of the different kinds of questions you can use and to help you improve your skill in the use of these questions. The expected outcome is improved instruction. To accomplish different purposes in instruction and to meet the diverse needs of students you will need a command of several different types of questions. In too many classrooms, the kinds of questions used are limited to a very few types. A question can arouse curiosity, stimulate mental activity, or it can assure boredom or drudgery. What will it be for you as a questioner? A well-conceived question, presented in a timely manner, is a useful means to clarify and expand thinking (Sund and Carin 1978). Effective teachers select questions that are most appropriate for the student and the situation or topic being explored. If a teacher uses the same questions for all students and all circumstances, productive interaction is unlikely. The selection of questions cannot be left to chance. Intuition is not a sound basis for decisions about the kinds of questions to use. Purposeful decisions need to be made about the kinds of questions to ask (Wilen 1986). These choices must be guided both by the abilities of the students and the purposes to be accomplished in instruction. Each student and situation is very different, requiring a good command of a wide range of questions. An in-depth understanding of the characteristics of and the potentials for different types of questions is a valuable teacher competency.

Teacher questions are the means used to communicate the elements of the subject matter. They provide guidance to what is to be done with information and how it is to be done (Hunkins 1976). Selecting mostly factual recall questions limits drastically the number of things students can do with information and is manipulative as well; the consequence is to build dependence in students. Students will not become self-sufficient when someone is always directing their thinking. This eliminates possibilities for critical and creative thinking. The most outstanding example of manipulative behavior is frequent use of "yes" or "no" questions (Sund and Carin 1978). These are questions that begin with an auxiliary verb (could, should, does, is, was, etc.).

Spontaneity is a desirable quality in questioning behavior; however, some key questions must be planned. To leave all questions to the moment at hand is an oversight. Questions that stimulate thinking require prior thought. Taking time to plan questions allows the teacher to consider concepts to be developed and individual differences in students. Goals to be achieved and ways to respond to answers given by students can also be considered. These factors cannot be contemplated during interaction with students. A teacher who plans questions in advance is more confident.

In a recent review of research on questioning, Gall (1984) reported that 80 percent of the questions used in classrooms asked students to do something other than think. The heavy emphasis on rote memory is well documented in the research for all instructional levels. This finding has been relatively stable for the last 70 years. The persistence of the view of teaching as imparting knowledge and learning as recalling and repeating information is the reason for the narrow choice of questions used in instruction (Wilen 1986).

Questions are used for numerous purposes. Some of these purposes include initiating discussion, reviewing material, guiding problem solving, diagnosing student abilities, evaluating student preparedness, controlling behavior, stimulating creative or critical thinking, and encouraging contributions. Other purposes might be clarifying misconceptions, supporting conceptual development, reinforcing understandings, and asking students to elaborate. It is very important to recognize that different kinds of questions are required for each of these purposes.

In this chapter, different kinds of questions from the cognitive and affective domains are examined. Both kinds are important if learning is to be functional and interesting; these two areas are mutually supportive. For every cognitive operation there is a complementary affective operation. In fact, some writers suggest that there is no separation between the domains. Not only do we want students to understand the subject matter but also we want them to be interested in it. To place emphasis on cognition alone, is to disregard questions that motivate students to be enthusiastic about their learning. It follows that as you improve your skill for identifying and using questions from the two domains, you will realize more positive results in your classroom. As you study the examples, consider how you could implement them in your classroom. Figure 4-1 is an illustration of the model used to guide your study of different kinds of questions. Keep in mind that division into categories is an arbitrary process but it is done so that the purposes of different kinds of questions can be clarified. This diagram is intended not only to illustrate the hierarchical arrangement of kinds of questions within each domain but also to show the horizontal relationships between the domains.

Figure 4-1. Model for Kinds of Cognitive and Affective Questions

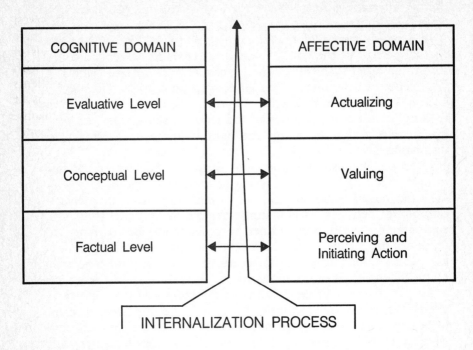

COGNITIVE DOMAIN

To be able to classify questions is basic to the construction and use of superior questions; however, it is only the first step. The challenge is to be able to create your own questions for each purpose; the even greater challenge is to use them appropriately in the classroom. Classifying has two useful purposes: (1) it helps the teacher make a distinction between questions that require minimal thinking and those that require complex thoughts, and (2) it helps the questioner to use questions more effectively. If you discover that a question gets poor results, this will give you cause to rephrase it or to look for better questions. Knowledge of a variety of questions gives one many more choices. Both the way the question is phrased and the intended level of thinking communicated in the question are important factors to consider when classifying questions. Your effectiveness as a questioner can depend on your ability to judge these qualities.

Factual Recall Questions

Questions at this level should be easy to identify. This is the lowest level and the type most frequently used in classroom interaction where students engage in frequent exercises of rote memory. These kinds of questions ask the student to remember specifics having to do with methods, processes, settings, and structure (Hunkins 1976). Students may also recall facts, observations, definitions, and ways or means of doing something. When responding to these kinds of questions, students might use such operations as naming, recalling, identifying, writing, listing, and distinguishing.

Examples of Factual Questions

What state produces the most wheat?

What is an illegal alien?

What is the correct procedure for appealing a court decision?

What is the pattern for birth rates among minority groups in this country?

What are the categories for rating motion pictures?

What criteria are used to determine poverty-level status?

If one wants to initialize a new floppy disc, what is the first step?

Conceptualization-Level Questions

Greater attention will be given to this level. Too little attention is given to the thinking required by these kinds of questions in classroom instruction. In this section, two types of questions are emphasized—convergent and divergent. One way to distinguish between kinds of questions is the degree to which they are open-ended. Generally, convergent questions are closed but more demanding than factual questions. They are narrow because there is little diversity in the responses solicited. One "best" answer is expected. By contrast, divergent questions create more possibilities for variety in the responses given and they provide the teacher with the means to be more of a facilitator of thinking.

For purposes of making distinctions between kinds of convergent and divergent questions the designations of "low" and "high" are used (Wilen 1986). This eliminates the confusion often associated with taxonomies wherein several different labels are used to classify questions.

71

By using fewer categories, we gain the advantages of both specificity and simplicity.

Low-Convergent Questions

Low-convergent questions do not lend themselves to the benefits identified with divergent questions. When a teacher is primarily concerned with "right" answers, these questions are more commonly used. Low-convergent questions are characteristic of those used in textbook materials. Regular use of these questions, without attention to other kinds as well, can hinder student development. Low-convergent questions call for transfer of information but in a predictable way (Intermediate Science Curriculum Study [ISCS] 1972). They require the student to put facts together and construct a response using operations such as comparing, contrasting, generalizing, transfering form, or explaining (Hunkins 1976). When a student responds to a low-convergent question, he/she must know certain facts, be able to associate these facts and give an explanation, usually in his or her own words. To state or explain relationships or explain concepts the respondent must use a higher level of thinking than recall. A student's response may involve knowledge of what is communicated and how to make use of it. Questions at this level will determine if the student is able to organize and select facts and ideas using information provided in the content under consideration. Stating the main ideas of material is also involved. The student may put knowledge to work by changing statements to another language form or by paraphrasing information. The student may also identify extensions, tendencies or trends to determine implications, consequences, corollaries, or effects as described in the original communication (Hunkins 1976).

Examples of Low-Convergent Questions

According to the textbook definition of revolution and our study of Central America, which conflicts in this area would be considered revolutions?

How would you use the directions provided in the resource materials to solve this problem?

You have heard two points of view about violence on television; how are these two perspectives similar?

After examining these two pictures that depict circus life, what similarities can be identified between the two scenes?

72

Using the statistics provided on the mortgage calculator chart and information provided in the article, what relationships can be noted between interest rates and housing starts?

What is the meaning conveyed in this cartoon about the state election for governor?

How would you say the phrase "You make your failure certain by being the first person to be convinced of it" in Spanish?

In your own words, describe how people misread the signs in the story "Alec's Song."

Identify and describe an example of cooperation between businesses in the community and the schools.

High-Convergent Questions

These are the kinds of questions that encourage students to reason. Consequently, they are important for critical thinking. Reasoning frequently does not occur without stimulation and direction from the teacher's questions. When students respond to these questions they will look for evidence to support, give reasons for behaviors or outcomes, and draw conclusions. They may break ideas, situations, or events down into their component parts. As they diagnose these elements, students look for motives for behaviors, unstated assumptions, cause and effect, and the relationships of elements to a total organizational scheme (Hunkins 1976). In so doing, students may distinguish between inferences, interpretations, and generalizations. They may develop their own and look for evidence to support them. These are questions that are used as probes to get students to extend their thinking by supporting assertions.

Examples of High-Convergent Questions

Why do you think violence on television appeals to so many people?

For what reasons do you think Americans attach so much importance to owning a pet?

After reading this article on teacher burnout, what evidence can you give that supports the contention the burnout may not be real?

Now that you have completed the sliders experiment, what can you conclude about the manipulation and control of variables?

What evidence can you give to support your position that unemployment is directly related to lack of education?

Why do you think the author of this article chose to use the title he did?

Why do you suppose that positive human relations are so difficult for people and governments?

What do you think are some reasons that people attach so much meaning to grades despite their negative effects?

Divergent Questions

Responses to divergent questions are less predictable than to those of convergent questions. In fact, as long as the response is given in a serious vein and represents an honest consideration of the facts or situation, there is considerable leeway regarding what constitutes an acceptable answer to a divergent question. The responses may be unknown to or not expected by the questioner. When a student responds to divergent questions he/she needs the freedom to generate unique, new, or imaginative ideas (ISCS 1972). For students to do the kind of thinking required by divergent questions, they must have an atmosphere where there is an opportunity to explore ideas without the constraints or the press to give ''correct'' answers. Initially, it may not be important for students to give ''right'' answers but to think broadly, to have the mental experience of exploring a variety of ideas (Sund and Carin 1978). If a teacher discovers that students lack information to deal adequately with open-ended questions, then narrower questions can be used to structure the missing knowledge base. Conceptual understanding can be enhanced through this process. In response to these questions, students might develop a plan of attack for a problem, propose solutions, or create a product. They may also speculate about possible outcomes or hypothesize from prior analyses (Hunkins 1976). Responses may take time to develop.

Low-Divergent Questions

Questions that ask the student to think of alternative ways to do something are different from those that require the student to synthesize a number of elements to create new or different ideas or to give some communication that is original. Actually, low-divergent questions might be one of the first steps in the problem-solving process or in a sequence of questions where the student brainstorms possible solutions.

74

What are some ways of dealing with the problem of the flood of illegal aliens into this country?

What are some ways workers replaced by robots or other new technologies might be helped to achieve a new employment status?

What are some ways to change the mass transit system in this city?

What are some approaches that could be used by the EPA to solve the problem of toxic waste dumps?

What are some different titles we might give to this story?

What are some ways that depictions of violence on television might be reduced?

High-Divergent Questions

High-divergent questions are the kinds of questions that encourage creative thinking, the kind that can motivate students to higher levels of thinking. These questions have students formulate generalizations and give diverse, original, or novel responses; however, research shows that only 5 percent of the questions used in classrooms are of this type. Respect for and confidence in students' abilities can be demonstrated in questioning patterns that incorporate appropriate use of high-divergent questions. This requires that teachers think of the content to be learned in different ways or that they create different contexts for learning required material other than the one characteristic of the traditional, factual mode. For high-divergent questions, students might do the following: elaborate, make divergent associations, point out implications, or do open predicting.

Examples of High-Divergent Questions

Suppose that you were placed in a position of authority, how would you deal with the problem of poor human relations?

Speculate on the future of the automobile industry in this country.

How would you plan a campaign to reduce the number of car thefts in this area?

What kind of a plan might be devised to reduce violence on television?

What kind of strategy might be employed to help the border patrol to deal effectively with the influx of illegal aliens?

What do you predict will happen when the legal drinking age is raised to 21?

75

What do you predict will happen if you use a heavier ball in the slider system experiment?

Suppose that you were suddenly stranded on a tropical island, how would you use the local materials to survive?

How might life in Russia be different if the Soviets had adopted capitalism?

Evaluative Questions

The evaluation level in its most complex form is a blend of all the other levels. However, evaluation questions can be as simple as factual questions. In a sense it is a kind of "floating" category (Gall, Dunning, and Weathersby 1971, p. 191). Even at the factual level, students are making judgments about the value of materials and methods. When students respond to evaluation questions they may express opinions, judge validity and merits of ideas or solutions, select against a set of values, make discriminations or take a self-selected position on an issue, or evaluate the quality of a product. They may also judge accuracy and consistency. Words or phrases commonly used with these questions are: in your opinion, what is most appropriate, do you agree, would it be better, rate, and which would you consider (Hunkins 1976).

One of the qualities of these questions that makes them higher order is the potential they offer for probing the student to support his/her response. In each of the examples listed below the teacher could respond to the student's answer with a probe—usually a *"why"* question that requests the student to support, to provide evidence, or to explain the position (opinion) he/she has taken (expressed). The nature of this probe would depend somewhat on whether the student answers in the affirmative or negative. If the student gives more than a yes or no response it is also helpful to give as feedback at least part of the student's own words in the probe. For example, the student's response to the first question might be: "No. I think 11:00 P.M. is too restrictive." Your probe might be: "Why do you think 11:00 P.M. is unrealistic?" Anticipate possible responses to each of the questions and see if you can think of probes you might use.

Examples of Evaluative Questions

Do you believe the curfew for teenagers is appropriate?

Do you think it is a good idea for the United States to intervene in the affairs of Central American and Carribbean countries?

Some people believe that when group homes for the mentally handicapped are located in a residential area the property values go down. Do you think this is true?

Which of the crafts made by the artist do you like best?

Given the choice between Japanese and American-made cars, what criteria would you use to make a choice about the car to buy?

In your opinion, should the state use the lottery as a source of funds to support education?

Do you agree that competition has more negative than positive effects?

It is helpful for a teacher to keep a record of the kinds of questions asked. This can lead to greater diversity in the interactions with students. Such a record will give the teacher information about the quality of the interaction and the extent to which he/she is listening to all students and not just to those who are requesting his/her attention. Both convergent and divergent questions can help the teacher assess whether a student knows what he/she is talking about with respect to the content of a lesson. This also becomes a way of determining the students' preparedness for learning or evaluations. Appropriate use of these kinds of questions offers a means of guiding the students' progress in the learning process (ISCS 1972). An observation form to record the cognitive levels of a teacher's questions is provided in Chapter 9.

SELF-TEST

Convergent and Divergent Questions

In the previous discussions, you were given examples of a variety of questions from different subject matter areas, for different instructional levels, and on diverse topics to give you some idea of a range of possibilities. Here a specific topic is used as a basis for identifying questions at the different levels to give you an idea of the variety possible with a single topic. At the same time you will be able to assess how much you have learned about the question types previously examined. To test your skill and to diagnose your understanding of convergent and divergent questions, read the paragraph and complete the self-test that follows. To do so, use the key shown after the information to identify each question by type.

Illegal Aliens

The flood of illegal aliens into the United States is increasing drastically and is almost out of control. The border patrol and other federal and local law enforcement agencies caught 900,000 "wetbacks" during the past year. Still, they speculate that they have captured only about 25 percent of those who have crossed the border. Mexico is the primary source of the problem because of its easy border access. However, in recent years larger and larger numbers have also been coming from other Central American and Carribbean countries. Organized groups are charging exorbitant fees to help enormous numbers of illegal aliens to find their way into this country. Because of the large numbers of American citizens of Hispanic origin and other factors characteristic of certain locales in this country, these illicit visitors can quickly blend into the population. They are locating in large cities throughout the country and in the Southwest and West in particular. They take on low-paying jobs and draw benefits from public service agencies. They often go without paying taxes. The number of groups, like labor unions, veterans, and the unemployed, who are protesting is increasing. Yet, the border patrol seems helpless to curb the tide. Recently, there was talk of using troops to guard the border. If this trend continues, it might lead to much tighter controls of entry into the United States for all peoples.

L–C   Low-Convergent
H–C   High-Convergent
L–D   Low-Divergent
H–C   High-Divergent

_____ 1. What relationships might be observed between this problem and other societal problems such as drug abuse?

_____ 2. Government officials and others are concerned with the "flood of illegal aliens." What does this phrase mean?

_____ 3. You have heard two points of view on this problem in the discussion. How are these two views similar?

_____ 4. If 900,000 illegal aliens are caught in one year and this represents 25 percent of the number, how many will have entered without getting caught after three years?

_____ 5. Compare the economic system of Mexico with that of the United States.

_____ 6. What are some of the conditions in Mexico and other countries that would motivate people to do this?

_____ 7. What evidence can you give to show that location of illegal aliens in cities creates a problem?

_____ 8. What are some ways that law enforcement officials might deal with this problem?

_____ 9. If the rate of influx of illegal aliens is to continue at its current level, what do you predict will be the problems of the future?

_____ 10. For what reasons might people from other countries want to come to the United States?

_____ 11. Considering the current economic crisis in Mexico and drawing on information read in your text, what are some conclusions you can draw?

_____ 12. What are some examples of illegal aliens coming from countries other than Mexico?

_____ 13. What are some strategies that the United States government might use to encourage the Mexican and other governments to take more action?

_____ 14. What kind of a plan would you devise to eliminate the problem?

_____ 15. Study the chart on the numbers of illegal aliens that are locating in cities. From this chart, which of the following judgments could be made? (A list to select from is provided.)

Key

Check your performance. If you do not correctly identify at least 12 items, it might be wise to review the descriptions and examples given in each of the previously discussed levels for questions.

1. H–C	6. H–C	11. L–C
2. L–C	7. H–C	12. L–C
3. L–C	8. L–D	13. H–D
4. L–C	9. H–D	14. H–D
5. L–C	10. H–C	15. L–C

AFFECTIVE DOMAIN

The emotions that each person experiences dramatically influence how he or she learns. Feelings, attitudes, appreciations, interests, and values emanate from experiences and the perceptions we have of ourselves (Krathwohl, Bloom, and Masia 1964). Using questions to draw attention to these affective responses and to clarify them will give more personal meaning to all learning. When students confront their emotions in the context of the subject matter, this adds to the significance of the learning experience. Teachers who use questions from the affective domain are helping students to work through the internalization of values and the conceptualization of a value system. This contributes to self-understanding and self-knowledge can result in a more positive self-esteem. Students who have positive self-esteem have fewer learning problems and approach learning more enthusiastically. To not consider cognitive and affective qualities simultaneously is a serious oversight.

Affective operations are a part of all learning. There is much research that shows that cognition and affect are inseparable, in fact, one may influence the other. As a person becomes more informed, interest is increased. Some argue that, if students are motivated to be interested in the subject matter, cognitive operations are more easily attained (Krathwohl, Bloom, and Masia 1964). Students cannot process information without some feeling for the materials and ideas examined. They display either a willingness or unwillingness to respond to the material. As students process information at different levels of cognition, they develop ownership and commitment to ideas. When this happens, feelings, attitudes, and beliefs surface. At the higher levels of thinking, questions that ask students to conceptualize and value are highly interrelated (Krathwohl, Bloom, and Masia 1964). At the lower levels, information gathering and awareness are also highly connected. If a teacher is able to recognize these linkages, it will be easier to identify questions appropriate for each domain and to use them in the same interaction (Hunkins 1976). These linkages will be clarified more extensively in the last section of this chapter.

In the discussion that follows, questions will be identified for three levels of questioning in the affective domain. The purpose will be to identify several models for you to consider and to think about how you might incorporate them into your instruction. In general, these levels describe a hierarchy. At the low end of the hierarchy, questions encourage students to express interests and appreciations; at the opposite end of the hierarchy are questions that require students to express established values and internalized value systems. The transitional or middle level of the hierarchy includes questions that have to do with attitudes and values. As a student moves through this internalization process, the locus of control for behavior changes from external to internal (Krathwohl, Bloom, and Masia 1964).

Perceiving and Initiating Action

Awareness and responsiveness are key prerequisites to all learning. At this first level of the internalization process, the teacher is using questions to sensitize the student and to stimulate the student's action on his/her environment. Questions at this level are designed to determine how much attention a student gives to stimuli. How willing is he/she to attend to them? How able is the student to focus his/her attention on selected phenomena and to do something with or about them? How willing is he/she to comply with the suggestions or encouragement of others? How motivated is he/she to take some kind of action? What is his/her emotional response (feelings) about a phenomenon? The purpose of these questions, then, would be to probe the interests and feelings toward a phenomenon that might be identified through experience and lower-cognitive questions (Hunkins 1976). It is important to help the student to see how he/she perceives environmental stimuli. Perception is influenced by experiences. Initial questions do not ask the student to make assessments (Krathwohl, Bloom, and Masia 1964). Questions used later in the internalization process determine how much of a commitment the student has or how strong an emotional response is given to stimuli. Consequently, the student may move from a position of neutrality to one of action. Although he/she may need to be encouraged initially to consider a phenomenon, eventually the student may seek it out and acquire satisfaction from engaging it.

Examples of Perceiving and Initiating Action Questions

1. Here are some pictures of people in the news today. Look at the pictures and say the first thing that comes to mind with each picture. (It might be occupation, basis of notoriety, name, etc.) Are you aware of who the people are that make the news? Do you recognize those people who are recognized in the news? (sensitizing to stimuli)

2. Below are the names of some television personalities. Identify each. Do you recognize them? Do you know these people? (sensitizing to stimuli)

81

3. You have just spent a day at the Museum of Science and Industry. Respond to these questions concerning your feelings about this field trip:

To what extent was the trip interesting to you?
Which display got you most involved?
How do you feel about the amount of time spent on the trip?
Would you like to make the trip again?
Which activities interested you the most?
Which experiences would you like to repeat?
How much do you feel you learned on the trip? (willingness to attend)

4. For recess time this week, these are some activities to be offered. Which would be your preference to start the week? Which do you prefer to do more than once? (focusing attention)

5. In the following list are some things people will choose to do during summer break. Using the following key, respond to each activity:

    N — No way would I do this
    P — Probably would not do it
    U — Unsure, maybe
    M — Might do this sometime
    Y — Yes, I would definitely do this

_____ a. Work in a nursing home with the elderly.
_____ b. Work in a summer camp for handicapped children.
_____ c. Write letters to friends in different parts of the country.
_____ d. Spend time relaxing. (complying with existing values)

6. On your way to class you observe a student and an outsider making a money-drug exchange. Which of the following would you do?

_____ Ignore it.
_____ Intervene and tell them it is illegal.
_____ Report it to the principal.
_____ Talk to the student afterwards.
_____ Report the outsider but not the student.

If the exchange were going on between two friends, how would you respond? Which of these things might you not do under any circumstances? (willingness to take action)

7. Complete these statements with your most immediate response or feeling:

The film *Vision Quest* made me feel that _____
The phrase "all men are created equal" makes me want to _____
Classical music _____
After watching the television program on the Holocaust, I _____
The cliché "better safe than sorry" makes me think _____ (expressing emotional response)

8. Construct a circle. Identify six kinds of things you do outside of school during the school week. Divide the circle into sections to show the percentage of time you spend on each. Are you satisfied with the way you use your time? (Raths, Harmin, and Simon 1966). (focusing attention)

Valuing Questions

What does it mean to value? Raths, Harmin, and Simon (1966) use the terms "choosing," "prizing," and "acting," to describe the valuing process. Krathwohl, Bloom, and Masia (1964), with certain qualifications, liken values to "beliefs" and "attitudes." In both perceptions of valuing, it is clear that when the student values, he/she is giving worth to objects, phenomena, or beliefs. The degree of attachment to a value depends on where the student is in his/her internalization of a value. At the lowest level of valuing, beliefs are expressed with less certainty because the learner has not developed a commitment to them (Krathwohl, Bloom, and Masia 1964). The teacher's questions would serve to help the student clarify how strongly he/she believes in the value. Consequently, the student subjects the value to more scrutiny at this level. As the value becomes more internalized he/she claims more ownership and begins to act in ways that are in keeping with the value. The student's behavior with regard to the value is likely to become more consistent. He/She acts with greater conviction in accordance with the value and is less conscious of the value because it has become an integral part of his/her behavior. Essentially, the student can be identified by the value as expressed in his/her beliefs and attitudes. At this point the behavior of the student is more guided by conscience. When the student arrives at a higher level of valuing, he/she seeks out stimuli related to the value, and a firm emotional acceptance (faith) is expressed in statements of belief. Demonstrations of loyalty are characteristic of this level of commitment to a value (Krathwohl et al. 1964). When the student is operating at this higher level, questions are used to determine the degree of commitment to beliefs. Questions also help the student identify activities that are indicative of a value position (Hunkins 1976). Questions reveal how actively involved the student is with the value. The operations required to respond to these questions are similar to those of the conceptual level in the cognitive domain.

Examples of Valuing Questions

1. How far would you go to win someone's friendship?

Would do anything even if it meant losing another friend	Would do nothing at all
1 ——————————— 8	(Cunningham 1977, p. 178)
(clarifies strength)	

2. Ask a series of thought-provoking questions for the purpose of stimulating value-related responses:

   a. Are you loyal to all your friends?
   b. Is there any circumstance when loyalty would be violated?
   c. Do you feel like you would be willing to donate parts of your body to a friend in need?
   d. Do you like people who stand up for their rights?
   e. Do you accept others' views even though they might conflict with yours?
   f. Do you feel responsible for the behavior of others?
   (ownership of value)

3. What actions have you taken on any of the activities listed below?

   Wrote a letter to a company to complain about a poor product.
   Called someone to congratulate her/him on some success or for something she/he did well.
   Attended a meeting for a community cause.
   Picketed peacefully for a cause.
   Organized a drive for a petition.
   Approached a city official about an issue or problem.
   (acting with conviction)

4. In the following, rank order people described according to whom you would most like to be like. Put the person you would least like to be like at the bottom of your list.

   A teacher who is buddy with students.
   A person who spends all his/her saved money to help someone else.
   A student who is very popular because he makes others feel good.
   A police officer who turns in a colleague for taking money.
   A person who has to have new clothes for every event.
   A teacher or parent who is very strict and requires adherence to rules no matter what the circumstances.
   An environmentalist who counts the sheets of toilet tissue.
   (seeking value and emotional acceptance)

5. You are stopped at a traffic light. The people in the car in front of you finish a fast food meal and throw their trash into the street. What would you do? (Student might choose from a list of alternatives). (behavior guided by value)

6. During a weekend you pass by the school. You observe people abusing the property. What would you do? (Student might choose from alternatives.) Would you be satisfied with that action? (behavior guided by value)

84

Actualizing Questions

Once the student has succeeded in internalizing values, experiences expose him/her to new values to process. The learner must evaluate or reconsider existing values in light of these new competing values. Consequently, the individual is forced to look at the relationships between values, to make choices, and to order values by giving priority to more dominant ones (Krathwohl et al. 1964). The result is the organization of values into a system that guides the person's behavior. Finally, the student has made adjustments in behavior that reflect an internally consistent system. His/Her behavior is in keeping with a well-established system of values. The value system becomes so operational as to be illustrative of a "philosophy of life" (Hunkins 1976). This is the culmination of the internalization process (Krathwohl et al. 1964). Established value systems enable the student to function effectively in different situations. Questions at this level reveal the essence of the individual in that he/she can be characterized by what is said, what is done, and by expressions of belief about the person's world (Hunkins 1976). Questions allow the person to take a stand and act from an established position. The total development of the student is exposed. Questions reveal the character of the student. The student comes to be able to answer the questions "Who am I?" and "What do I stand for?" (Krathwohl, Bloom, and Masia 1964). Interactions between this level and the cognitive levels of conceptualization and evaluation are common because of the similarity of the operations involved.

Examples of Actualizing Questions

1. "The following list consists of statements made by other members of the class. Each statement shows some thing or things the owner values. Identify the names of class members with these statements." (Sanders 1966, p. 181) (relating)

2. The story just read presented several value positions. Indicate those values that agree with your values or that contrast with what you value. (naming choices)

3. In our discussion of the personal problem you identified Friday, what do you see as some of the things that are limitations for you in solving the problem? (ordering values)

4. When you hear the song "We Are the People," what statement best describes your feeling?

_____ Sympathy
_____ Pride
_____ Concern
_____ Understanding

Why do you feel this way? (ordering values)

5. With regard to the following list of ways to help the poor and/or the homeless of the country, which would you support? What would you do privately to help the handicapped? (internally consistent system)

6. Which of the following sets of beliefs best characterizes your philosophy of life? (internally consistent system)

7. In the description of life positions, which one most closely matches the life position for which you strive? (internally consistent system)

8. Of the following list of statements, which demonstrates what you consider to be the basic purpose of life? (internally consistent system)

It should be apparent to you that questions in the affective domain are more difficult to classify and construct than those of the cognitive domain. This is probably because of the complexity of the domain but may be so more because of our lack of attention to and experiences with this domain (Hunkins 1976). Just as practice and analysis of questions was important to cognition, so it is with affect. The primary purpose of affective questions is not to direct students' answers but to help them understand how they believe and function, and why they do it the way they do. Affective questions are more concerned with having students process interests, appreciations, beliefs, and attitudes than with information. By using affective questions along with cognitive questions, students will gain greater focus, both as to what they know and think, as well as to how they feel about, believe, and value an area of study.

COORDINATING THE DOMAINS

It was suggested that the linkages between the cognitive and affective domains are direct, and some strong statements were made about the importance of these crossovers. An issue was also made of the importance of the teacher's ability to recognize and use these relationships between the two domains for questions. These connections are illustrated in this section. Of even greater importance is the need to give attention to both affect and cognition during the teaching/learning process. Here we seek to capture the overlap by illustrating relationships and by providing examples of how questions from both domains might be used simultaneously. The topic of substance abuse is used as a basis for illustrating examples of related questions.

How the domains are used to plan and carry out instruction is a useful basis for considering their relationships. Most often the cognitive domain is used to set the stage for the affective domain (Krathwohl, Bloom, and Masia 1964). We provide students with information for the purpose of influencing their attitudes. A perceptive teacher uses questions to solicit cognitive behaviors to move the students toward accomplishing affective operations and/or outcomes. Much of what we think of as "good teaching" is the teacher's ability to capture the interest of students by using cognitive questions to get students to consider and explore concepts that have both cognitive and affective qualities to them (Krathwohl, Bloom, and Masia 1964). This is further enhanced by challenging the students' entrenched beliefs and creating discussions where they have the opportunity to confront issues head-on.

Effective teachers use an interest-grabbing strategy to begin question-answer or discussion periods. They often develop interests in material so that the student will be more inclined to use the information learned. Motivation is critical to learning. This is a way to use the affective domain to set the stage for cognitive operations. A positive challenge to drives and emotions can be one of the primary means for giving meaning to cognitive activities. "Effective instruction uses interest-capturing behavior to intrigue the student, creating the motivation to inquire and to learn the subject matter" (Krathwohl, Bloom, and Masia 1964, p. 58).

Close analysis of the domains reveals that affective explorations interspersed with cognitive tasks provide a transition from one cognitive task to the next. Krathwohl, Bloom, and Masia (1964) liken this process to a person climbing to a designated height using two ladders, one beside the other but arranged so that the rungs of one ladder are between the rungs of the other. Achieving the desired end point is accomplished by alternately climbing a rung on one ladder and then the rung on the next ladder. Thus alternating between affective and cognitive domains, one may seek a cognitive goal using the attainment of an affective outcome or vice versa. Clearly, one serves the purpose of the other.

As noted earlier, examination of the levels within each domain reveals some relationships across levels. These ties are most evident at the lowest and highest levels. Perceiving a phenomenon is necessary to knowing it. Only when one pays attention to a stimulus will one learn about it. At the upper levels of the affective domain, valuing and actualizing, the response behaviors are, at least, in part cognitive (Krathwohl, Bloom, and Masia 1964). The student has to be able to conceptualize values to process them and to organize them into a system that is useful to him or her. To organize values and to integrate them into a system demands using the cognitive operations demonstrated in high-convergent responses. High-divergent operations are used as the student deals with new values and value complexes by synthesizing the new into existing values. To balance values against one another, the student calls on evaluative operations from the cognitive domain. Therefore, to facilitate these affective operations a teacher will use questions from several levels of the cognitive domain as well as appropriate affective questions. "To make precise linkages between the two domains is not the point; rather, the central focus is for the teacher to realize that when generating questions in one domain, he or she is also stimulating responses and questions in the other" (Hunkins 1976, p. 68). An illustration of the integration of questions among levels within a domain and across domains is presented in the next section, using the topic of "Substance Abuse" as a stimulus.

Substance abuse is not only a serious societal problem but one that plagues school settings. It is chosen as a basis for illustrating parallels and crossovers between the two domains because it is a topic that has much potential for both cognitive and affective considerations. Examples are not intended to show exact linkages in terms of content but more so in terms of operations the student performs when responding to questions from the different levels within the cognitive and affective domains. The examples that follow are intended to show three relationships: factual and low-convergent to perceiving and initiating action; conceptual to valuing; and evaluative to actualizing. In reality there may be more complex crossovers between the domains. It is simplified here to make a point. Note that these examples are arranged in clusters to make comparisons. The first cluster includes factual, low-convergent, and perceiving examples. The second and third clusters consist of conceptual and valuing, and evaluative and actualizing questions, respectively. Vertical relationships across clusters can also be identified.

Factual Level

1. "Which of the following substances is not known as a narcotic?
   a. heroin
   b. marijuana
   c. morphine
   d. methadone" (Dacey 1986, p. 342)
2. What is the chemical substance in marijuana that is so dangerous?
3. Based on the handbook on drugs and drug abuse, what are three things you can do to avoid getting hooked on drugs?
4. "How do most drug users make their first contact with illicit drugs?
   a. through 'pushers'
   b. through their friends
   c. accidentally
   d. through the media" (Dacey 1986, p. 342)

Low-Convergent

1. What are some examples of different classes of drugs?
2. Explain in your own words how mood-modifying drugs affect behavior.
3. After studying the statistics from the chart about antisocial behavior comparing users with nonusers, what differences can you note?
4. How do you explain the influence of peer pressure in the drug problem?

Perceiving and Initiating Action

1. Below is a list of commonly abused substances and a list of effects. Match the substances in each case with an effect.
2. Below is a list of true statements about substance abuse. Place a check mark beside those that are surprising to you; put an X beside those that give you cause for concern; and put a V beside those about which you would like to know more.
3. What activities are you interested in doing that are free of pressures by other students to do things a certain way?
4. Are you aware that most drug users make their first contact with illicit drugs through their friends?

Conceptual Level

1. What are some of the reasons people would succumb to the pressures to engage in substance abuse?
2. If you wanted to argue the case against substance abuse, what are some main points you would make?

3. What kind of a plan could be used to create a school atmosphere that would encourage students to resist experimenting with drugs?

4. What evidence is there to support the importance of the family and family relationships in creating an atmosphere that discourages drug abuse?

5. What are some of the reasons people might give for not abusing drugs?

6. What are some ways in which the adults and students in your school could work together to eliminate a drug problem?

7. Create a poster that communicates the message about the dangers of substance abuse.

8. Why do you suppose that alcohol use has become such a problem among adolescents?

9. What are some ways that a child of an alcoholic parent could be helped to cope with the situation?

Valuing Level

1. Do you have a responsibility to prevent friends who are under the influence of alcohol from driving?

2. What actions have you taken to resist pressures to use drugs?

3. Do you feel responsible for changing the conditions that contribute to a drug problem in your school?

Never Under Any   Try
   Circumstances   Anything
      1 _____ 8

4. Have you contributed to—

_____ planned events that encourage school unity?
_____ a student group against drunk driving?
_____ a campaign to reduce substance abuse in your school?
_____ a study of alcohol as a problem in your school?
_____ improving relations with potential drug users?
_____ a program to make students better informed about substance abuse?
_____ activities to improve relations with your family members?

5. A friend of yours disagrees with others about the dangers of alcohol use. Which of the following should be done?

_____ have him/her attend an AA meeting
_____ participate in a discussion with recovering alcoholics
_____ see a film on alcoholism
_____ provide him/her with statistics on alcohol as a problem
_____ call attention to those things that cause people to use alcohol as an escape

6. Suppose you have a friend who shoplifts to support a drug habit, what would you do?

7. Rank order the following list of people from the most acceptable to least acceptable:

_____ drug pusher
_____ a friend who reports a student using drugs
_____ a student who rejects the pressures of others to use drugs
_____ a student who reports a drug pusher
_____ a police officer who goes undercover to catch drug users
_____ a friend who uses drugs only once in awhile and stays within certain limits

Evaluative Level

1. Do you consider substance abuse to be America's most serious societal problem? If not, what are some more critical problems? (Sanders 1966)
2. Do you believe that people who experiment with less harmful drugs will eventually try more harmful drugs?
3. Some people believe that marijuana is a harmless drug. Do you agree with this belief?
4. Do you think there is a relationship between substance abuse and the number of hours spent watching television?
5. Do you think alcoholic parents will transmit their habits to their children?
6. Some people who abstain from abusing drugs give religious or moral reasons for doing so. How do you feel about the soundness of these as a rationale for avoiding involvement?

Actualizing Level

1. Which of the following sets of beliefs best characterizes your philosophy of life as it encompasses the choice to use or not use chemical substances?

_____ To intervene is an infringement on individual rights.
_____ People do not have the freedom of choice when it comes to substance abuse because of the dangers it presents to others.
_____ The magnitude of the substance-abuse problem is only a mirror image of the ills of an open society.
_____ It's a communist plot to undermine the American way of life.
_____ It reflects the inability of schools to teach the decision-making skills and to build emotional stability in students.
_____ The magnitude of the problem only reflects the declining importance of the family in this society.
_____ The problem demonstrates that we put making money above humanistic concerns in this society.
_____ The United States far outdistances other countries in the world in the magnitude of this problem because there are too many pressures.

91

2. Which of the phrases listed below express what you believe to be the basic purpose of life or your main life goal? (Hunkins 1976; Krathwohl, Bloom, and Masia 1964):

_____ maintain positive family relations
_____ sustain a strong religious orientation
_____ be happy
_____ accomplish success through material wealth
_____ succeed through achievement of power
_____ accomplish security
_____ adaptability
_____ contributing to the happiness and welfare of others
_____ carrying out my duties
_____ living God's will
_____ protection against adversity
_____ finding my niche in life
_____ surviving life's problems
_____ living for the joy of the moment

3. Do you think substance abuse destroys one's desire to achieve and assures failure in life?

In this chapter you were given examples of some parallels for kinds of questions across levels within the cognitive domain (conceptual, factual, and evaluative) and the affective domain (valuing, perceiving, and actualizing), and linkages across the domains (conceptual to valuing, factual to perceiving, and evaluating to actualizing) were illustrated. The purpose was to demonstrate the relationships between the cognitive and affective domains. By way of example, you were shown how questions from one domain serve the purposes of the other domain. Is it clear that it is important to use questions from both domains in discussions? In reality they are integrated with one another. You have had an opportunity to see and classify examples. Your challenge now will be to construct your own questions, implement them in class discussions, and achieve balance in the kinds of questions you ask of students. A balance of questions between levels within a domain gives your students the benefits of thinking about and processing information in different ways. Creative and critical thinking can be two desirable outcomes. Achieving a balance in questioning across the domains is even more important. This gives students the opportunity to personalize learned material, to express their emotions, and to relate it more to their own life experiences. For you to make learning a rich and fulfilling activity for both you and your students, a variety of questions from all levels and both the cognitive and affective domains is desirable.

SUMMARY

Hopefully, you have seen the excitement a "little bit of difference" makes in a well-formulated question. Now, you can experience this excitement by experimenting with these kinds of questions in your classroom discussions. As you gain more experience, you will discover other ways to improve your questions. One really never arrives. Revision is an ongoing process. The cognitive abilities and values of students are constantly changing; to be effective you will find it necessary to be responsive to these changes. You have the background to achieve quality. Your students are counting on you. What will you do about it? You can make your classroom a more exciting place in which to learn with the right kinds of questions. *The challenge is yours!*

REFERENCES

The content of this chapter is adapted from the works of Bloom; Aschner and Gallagher; Krathwohl, Bloom, and Masia; and the interpretations of their writing in this area and its application to questions and questioning by Hunkins.

Bloom, B. S., et al., eds. *Taxonomy of Educational Objectives, Handbook I: Cognitive Domain.* New York: David McKay, 1956.

Cunningham, R. T. "Questioning Behavior, or, How Are You at P.R.?" In *Implementing Teacher Competencies: Positive Approaches to Personalizing Education*, edited by J. W. Weigand. Englewood Cliffs, N.J.: Prentice-Hall, 1977.

Dacey, J. S. *Adolescents Today.* Glenview, Ill.: Scott, Foresman and Company, 1986.

Gall, M. "Synthesis of Research on Teachers' Questioning." *Educational Leadership* (November 1984): 40-47.

Gall, M. D.; Dunning, B.; and Weathersby, R. *Higher Cognitive Questioning: Minicourse Nine, Teacher's Handbook.* Beverly Hills, Calif.: Macmillan Educational Services, 1971.

Gallagher, J. J. *Productive Thinking of Gifted Children.* U.S. Office of Education, Department of Health, Education and Welfare, Cooperation Research Project No. 965. Urbana: University of Illinois, 1965.

Gallagher, J. J., and Aschner, M. J. "A Preliminary Report in Analysis of Classroom Interaction." *Merrill-Palmer Quarterly* 9 (1963): 183-94.

Hunkins, F. P. *Involving Students in Questioning*. Boston: Allyn and Bacon, 1976.

Intermediate Science Curriculum Study (ISCS). *Questioning*. Morristown, N.J.: Silver Burdett General Learning Corporation, 1972.

Krathwohl, D. R.; Bloom, B. S.; and Masia, B. B. *Taxonomy of Educational Objectives. The Classification of Educational Goals, Handbook II: Affective Domain*. New York: David McKay, 1964.

Raths, L. E.; Harmin, M.; and Simon, S. B. *Values and Teaching*. Columbus, Ohio: Charles E. Merrill, 1966.

Sanders, N.M. *Classroom Questions: What Kinds?* New York: Harper and Row, 1966.

Sund, R. B., and Carin, A. *Creative Questioning and Sensitive Listening Techniques: A Self Concept Approach*. Columbus, Ohio: Charles E. Merrill, 1978.

Wilen, W. W. *Questioning Skills, for Teachers*. 2d ed. Washington, D.C.: National Education Association, 1986.

5. USING WAIT TIME TO STIMULATE INQUIRY

by Mary Budd Rowe, Professor of Science Education, University of Florida, Gainesville

Consultants: Eve Singleton, P. K. Yonge Laboratory School, University of Florida, Gainesville; and Marianne E. Pennello, American Schools of The Hague Elementary School, the Netherlands

Teachers can become more productive inquirers by extending their pauses after asking questions and receiving responses from students. As wait time is extended, research shows that the quantity and quality of students' responses increase. The effects of extended wait time on students and teachers are presented, along with common verbal habits that interfere with wait-time results. Increased wait time provides students with an opportunity to think, essential in any inquiry-centered program. A cycle of inquiry is presented for teachers to help students organize their thoughts and convictions related to any major topic.

Thunder roared like the king of the sky.
It made me wonder . . .
    What made the lightning fly?
    where was the rain before it fell?

It made me wonder about myself,
Wonder who I was and would be.
Could I write a poem or a book?
Would my own work have value?
Would I have value without my work?

    And then the teacher said:
    "Are you daydreaming again?
    How many times must you be told?
    Pay attention to what I'm saying.
    Sit up straight and face the front.
    You haven't heard one word I've said.
    Won't you be sorry when you can't answer the
        questions on my test!"

It was a long time, Lord,
Before I wondered my rainy day questions again.

INTRODUCTION

What a dilemma we face as teachers today! We know full well that to really educate we must tap into the agenda of questions students have. At the same time, in these days we are increasingly being driven to gallop through content madly covering the questions we think may be on some third-party test. Where is the conversation out of which we build deeper understandings and values to take place, if not in the classroom? In our race to cover the text, if we leave too little room for inquiry, for wondering, for evaluating alternatives, for discussing student agendas, we may convert our students into adversaries unsuited for participation in a democracy. That is not a risk that we can afford.

If a conservationist, a geologist, a housing contractor, and a child cross a field together, it is unlikely that they will report the same observations when they reach the other side. Their different perspectives, concepts, and values cause each one of them to focus selectively on some interactions and to ignore others. We can only know the nature and quality of experience that each one had by listening to what they tell us about it and hearing them discuss their ideas with each other. Similarly, in the classroom the collective experience will be richer through sharing, comparing, and evaluating observations and inferences. In what follows, a distinction is drawn between inquisition and inquiry/conversation. Then a pausing technique is described that nurtures conversation/inquiry, which produces better test achievement on the management of complex ideas. This technique also prompts more productive questioning by both students and teachers. We, as well as our students, can become more productive inquirers, but like the people who crossed the field, we will be attending to different phenomena and making different stories out of our experience.

A PAUSE THAT REFRESHES: WAIT TIME

How long do you think you wait after you ask a question for students to begin an answer? (wait time 1)

After students give you an answer, how long do you wait for further explanation or elaboration? (wait time 2)

Most teachers, regardless of subject matter or grade level, have wait time 1 and wait time 2 pauses of one second or less if they have not had training on this variable. By simply increasing the average wait time 1 and 2 to *three seconds* or longer, you can produce marked changes both in student dialog and in your own patterns of responding. You have to judge for yourself whether you regard the outcomes listed below as desirable (Rowe 1978, Chapt. 9).

Effects of Extended Wait Times on Students

1. The length of student responses increased between 300 and 700 percent, in some cases more. Normally students offer the least target possible. Wait time 2 is particularly powerful in prompting elaboration. This effect is as pronounced for kindergarten and primary school (see, e.g., McKay 1985; Hanna 1977; Rowe 1974a) as it is for elementary (e.g., Rowe 1974b; Korinek 1985) and various high school subjects (e.g. in science, Rowe 1974b; Atwood and Stevens 1976; in social studies, Honea 1981; in second language learning, Shrum 1985. For a general review of research on wait time, see Rowe 1986).

2. Students are more likely to support inference statements by use of evidence and logic based on evidence.

3. Students do more speculating about possible alternative explanations or ways of thinking about a topic.

4. The number of questions asked by students increases. In the case of science, they propose more experiments. (Experiments are a way of asking questions of nature.)

5. Failures to respond decrease. It turns out that we tend to give slightly less time to students for whom we have the lowest expectations. When wait time 2 increases, we get more responses and richer responses. Here we see the dilemma of both students and teachers. Consider the teacher who said, "I am afraid that if I wait longer, the class will get out of control. Everyone wants to talk. There is no time to wait." Then hear a fifth grader, "I thought as fast as I could, but he didn't let me finish. I don't think anybody cares what I really think about anything."

6. Disciplinary moves decrease. Longer wait times may influence perception of caring and thus change motivation for productive participation. Students maintained on a rapid inquisitorial pattern show signs of restlessness and make attempts to withdraw or disrupt the process sooner than do students on a lower question

97

bombardment schedule. Under the more usual one second pausing pattern, most teachers ask between three and five questions per minute—some may ask as many as ten questions per minute. That means in an average 40-minute period students may have to respond to 120 or more questions. In such circumstances, it is not altogether surprising that teachers and students sometimes turn into adversaries—"It's the inquisitors versus the prisoners" as one social studies student put it.

7. Student-student exchanges increase and cooperation increases. This outcome is particularly influenced by wait time 2, which is the sum of all those pauses in student speech until the teacher joins the exchange again.

8. The variety of students participating voluntarily in discussions increases as does the number of unsolicited, but appropriate contributions. With extended wait times you simply do not have to ask as many questions as you otherwise might. The information that comes from students spontaneously makes more than half of all the questions teachers normally ask unnecessary. Moreover, there is a wider array of students who participate voluntarily— more students do more task-related talking. Some, who for all intents and purposes have been "invisible," suddenly become visible—and valuable!

9. Students gain confidence in their ability to construct explanations and to challenge the logic of a situation. This is reflected in fewer inflected responses, for example, statements that end on a question mark tone as though asking, "Is that what you want?"

10. Achievement on written measures improves, particularly on items that are cognitively more complex (see, e.g., Yeany and Porter 1982; Tobin 1984).

Effects of Extended Wait Time 1 and 2 on Teachers

1. Teacher responses exhibit greater flexibility—more facility at following the reasoning of students and using it to develop ideas.

2. The number and kinds of questions asked by teachers change. With the extended wait times, we hear more ideas and it is not necessary to ask as many questions as previously. The pattern of questions and comments changes and the teacher-student exchange

98

begins to sound more like a conversation. Apparently because we hear more from the students, we are more attuned to trying to understand their reasoning, and tend to invite more clarification or elaboration on their part; that is, we move up Bloom's taxonomy rather naturally (see Riley 1980).

3. Expectations for performance of certain students seem to improve. As a wider array of students participate voluntarily and get more practice at speaking whole ideas, expectations change gradually for both teachers and some of the students. This is often signaled by the teacher in such remarks as, "He never contributed like that before. Maybe he has a special 'thing' for this topic." And there is the third grader who said, "She only asks me easy questions—she doesn't think I can do the hard ones because I'm dumb. I wish there were some way nobody would ask me any questions. Why does school have to be just one question after another?"

Verbal Habits That Interfere with Wait-Time Results

In our eagerness to prompt responses from students, we may inadvertently create additional mental hazards for them. The verbal signals listed below not only interfere with wait time 2, the more important interval of the two wait times, but they carry unwanted implicit messages to students.

1. "Think!"
   We often rush in with such commands before the minimum three seconds of wait. While vague commands like "Think!" or "Put on your thinking cap!" often reflect the exasperation of an anxious adult, they are of little use to the students. Specific cues or, even better, an invitation to *ask* questions results in a better response.

2. Mimicry.
   Many teachers have developed the habit of repeating some or all of a student's answers. This mimicry often begins before the desirable wait time 2 interval of three seconds has passed. Moreover, it carries two implicit messages to students: there is no payoff for listening to each other or trying to evaluate what they say since the tone of the teacher will tell which answers are acceptable and which are not; the teacher is not only in control of behavior but of ideas as well. In fact, the widespread habit of mimicry may reflect teachers' concerns about control of behavior. Insofar as it cuts short

99

wait time 2 and the elaboration of ideas, it degrades the quality of student discourse. Extended wait time and the removal of mimicry improve both the discourse and the behavior. (See item 6 above.)

3. "Yes ... but ..." and "... though" constructions.
Although the pattern of mimicry rarely appears when adults speak to each other, the "Yes ... but ..." and "...though" constructions do appear, particularly when views diverge. If in a discussion you get a feeling of "no progress" or even vague irritation, there is a good probability that these two negative signals are sprinkled liberally through the discourse of one or more of the speakers. They imply an impending rejection or negation of an idea without sufficient consideration. They signal that the speaker who uses them does not receive and explore the new ideas but is bent on countering them. For students, swimming upstream against a conversation flow full of "Yes ... but ..." and "... though" constructions is like being part of salmon migration—only the hardiest survive the first few barriers; the rest drop out.

4. "Isn't it?" and "Right?"
These are devices that produce intellectual compliance—at least on the surface. The teacher makes some kind of statement, for example, in an experiment, "It's the ice that's doing it, isn't it?" (Notice the two uses of "it" in the statement. What are their referents?) Even if you don't know, as a student you know to say "Yes," but we fail to learn what he or she thinks or knows about the situation. The phrase "Right?" attached to a statement has a similar effect.

5. "Don't you think that ... ?"
This is another phrase, couched as a question, that makes it difficult for the other speaker to voice a contrary opinion. Its implicit message is the answer "yes," although that may not have been what the teacher intended. Try, instead, "What do you think?"

INQUIRY VERSUS INQUISITION

It takes time to study natural phenomena in science, to tease out the threads in social studies, to dig the meanings out of literature, to decide

100

how to attack a problem in mathematics, to plan and to ask questions. We did not achieve our present state of knowledge overnight, and neither will our students. If many students observe and think about the same problem, you can be certain that if you listen to them and they listen to each other, the richness of their observation and explanations will exceed your wildest imaginings. If students listen to each other, they may find themselves in disagreement when it comes to inferences and consequences of possible actions. To settle their differences, they must frequently reconsider the evidence and evaluate the arguments—indeed the science professions thrive on this process. But if we are to develop some skill in inquiry, teachers and students must give each other time to think and encouragement to do so. There is a distinction between inquiry and inquisition. Inquiry is something teachers and students may do together. Inquisition is something teachers do to students.

A Game Model of the Classroom

For the moment, imagine the classroom as a two-player game. The teacher is one player and the set of all the students is the other player. Imagine that each player can make the following four kinds of moves:

1. *Structuring*, in which a player gives directions, states procedures, or suggests changes ("What would happen if we put the thermometer in the ice water?").

2. *Soliciting*, in which a player asks a question ("What are the reasons this city is losing population?").

3. *Responding*, in which a player answers a question, expands on a structuring move, reports data, or continues a line of reasoning ("I predicted the temperature would fall lower than it did.").

4. *Reacting*, in which a player evaluates statements made by another ("Good," "Fine," "OK," "That doesn't work that way because ...").

In theory both players have equal access to all four moves. In practice the data show that teachers monopolize all except the responding move. With extended wait time there begins to be more sharing of the moves between the players; for example, students take on more structuring, reacting, and soliciting functions.

101

Rewards and Risk Taking

Inquiry programs depend heavily on an intrinsic rather than an extrinsic motivation model. Conceptual conflict is meant to drive inquiry along. Conversation marked by the free exchange of ideas is a mark of an inquiry-centered program. It is in preserving for ourselves and our students the "right to be wrong" that we gain courage to try out new ideas, to explore more alternatives, to evaluate objectively our own work as well as that of others. The authority for changing ideas comes from the results of experiments and discussions. Students have to learn to trust their ability to find and evaluate answers. To do that they have to feel safe in asking questions. They need time to think and an environment that encourages speculation. It is important to note that as much as 20 percent of the talk of some teachers consists of highly evaluative, nonspecific responses such as "Good," "Fine," "OK," or "You know better than that," statements that emphasize a success-failure perspective and take from students their opportunity to evaluate solutions based on evidence and logic or other features of the situation. So we need to reduce the flow of praise. When we do that, student confidence increases as does conceptual risk taking. (Rowe 1974b; and 1974c, which discusses rewards in the context of equity theory).

To improve the quality of student inquiry, we have to ask what are their ways of knowing and how do they get their information. Why do they believe what they do? It appears that their mode of getting information from the teacher is to listen and take what comes. Generally, they do not interrogate their teachers unless we make it safe for them to do so. They may turn to books if they are desperate. They get information from their peers by initiating a conversation outside class. Sometimes they will talk to parents or librarians.

Blending Their Agendas with Ours—A Cycle of Inquiry

It is possible to teach students how to inventory the state and stage of their thinking and convictions on any major topic by engaging them in a cycle of inquiry that has four components (see Figure 5-1): *Ways of Knowing, Actions/Applications* (students call this the "so what?" box), *Consequences*, and *Values* (Rowe 1983). Real inquiry, as opposed to contrived inquiry, generally begins with the action box and includes the extrapolation (thinking ahead) on consequences of particular actions and deciding whether the results are worth the effort or cost or disruption of

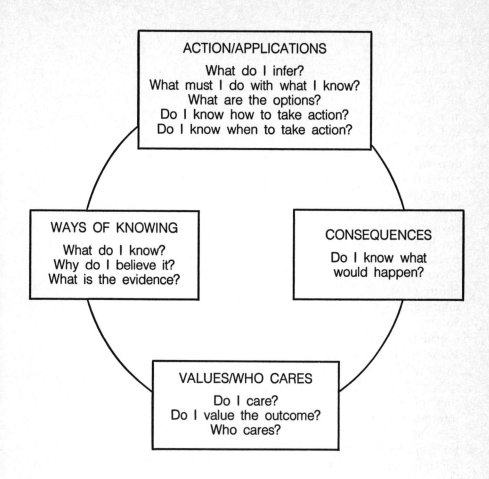

Figure 5-1. A Full Inquiry Cycle

SOURCE: "Science Education: A Framework for Decision Makers," by M. B. Rowe, *Daedalus* 112, 1983, p. 2.

the status quo. Unfortunately, we often confine formal experience in school to the Ways of Knowing box and then only to the first question, checking what students know. Students need to be challenged to examine evidence and to evaluate their grounds for belief. Only rarely do we invite and encourage them to examine what to do with what they know and how to do it or how to find out if it worked; namely, to enter the remaining three boxes in the cycle of inquiry. To do that they have to talk content, argue, and test ideas.

With the onset of pubescence, adolescents in every country begin to develop a world view, a nexus of beliefs that ultimately influences how they conduct their lives. There are 12 questions that crop up in one form or another among these young people all over the world. From observation, personal experience, and by talking seriously with anyone who will converse with them (as opposed to interrogating them), they form their own set of answers to these questions:

1. What kind of country is this?
2. What values control activities?
3. Where do I fit in?
4. Do they expect me to succeed or fail?
5. How much effort do I need to make?
6. Is success worth the effort?
7. Can I get help?
8. Do I have the energy and endurance?
9. What happens if I do not make the effort?
10. What am I up against? What is the competition?
11. What difference can I make?
12. Do I care? Does anybody care?

What does our way of presenting ideas contribute to their search for answers? How we teach matters. Increasing wait times and switching from inquisition to inquiry are two techniques that provide mental and emotional space for growth. If we work our way around the cycle (Figure 5-1) a few times each year, we make progress on their agenda as well as our own.

WHY TRY?

This social experiment called democracy depends in part for its survival on our ability to help students form wise answers to their questions. If we don't hear them, we can't help them. If we don't take the time, we fail in our most important responsibility and we cannot afford the consequences. Listen to Gwen Frostic, the poet and artist from Michigan:

We must not turn backward
    to find our way
but by persistence
and insistence
        engineer creative procedures
            that will not include destruction . . .
Let no one deny the problem
    nor dare to say
    it is not his
he is the plague of all mankind . . .
as individuals
    we must seek a new consciousness
    we are not spectators
        the fight is ours
        now. . . .

NOTES

It is not easy for most people to achieve extended wait times 1 and 2 without considerable practice. Make tape recordings of ten-minute segments of class discussion. Transcribe. Measure wait time 1 every time it occurs. To measure wait time 2, you sum up all the pauses that take place in student speech and between student speakers before you get back in the conversation. Transcribing is a laborious process but it seems to be the most effective way of focusing attention on the pauses and the changes they produce in student talk.

For elaboration on the ideas that are connected in this chapter and for more information on how to put them into practice, see Rowe, M. B., *Teaching Science as Continuous Inquiry*, Chapters 9 through 12 (New York: McGraw-Hill, 1978).

For a fuller listing of research reports, see Rowe, M. B. "Wait Time: Slowing Down May Be a Way of Speeding Up." *Journal of Teacher Education* (January-February 1986): 43-49. This paper also lists research on training people to extend wait times.

REFERENCES

Atwood, R. K., and Stevens, J. T. "Relationships Among Question Level, Response Level and Lapse Time: Secondary Science." *School Science and Mathematics* 76 (1976): 249-54.

Frostic, G. *Beyond Time*. Benzonia, Mich.: Presscraft Papers, 1971.

Hanna, G. P. "The Effect of Wait Time on the Quality of Response of First Grade Children." Master's thesis, University of Kansas, Lawrence, July 1977.

Honea, J. M. An Investigation of the Influence of Wait Time on Student Attitudes Toward Selected Social Studies Topics." Ph.D. diss., University of Houston. *Dissertation Abstracts International* 41, no. 9 (1981): 3858-A.

Korinek, L. "Teacher Questioning Strategies Used with Elementary Level Mildly Handicapped Students." Ph.D. diss., University of Florida, 1985.

McKay, M. J. "The Effect of Extended Teacher Wait Time on the Verbal Interactions Among Kindergarten Students and Teachers and on Student Achievement During Listening Comprehension Instruction." Ph.D. diss., The University of South Florida, 1985.

Riley, J. P. II. "The Effects of Teachers' Wait Time and Cognitive Question Level on Pupil Science Achievement." Paper presented at annual meeting of National Association for Research in Science Teaching, Boston, April 1980.

Rowe, M. B. "Pausing Phenomena: Influence on the Quality of Instruction." *Journal of Psycholinguistic Research* 3, no. 3 (1974c): 203-23.

_____. "Relation of Wait Time and Rewards to the Development of Language, Logic, and Fate Control: Part One—Wait Time." *Journal of Research in Science Teaching* 11, no. 2 (1974a): 81-94.

_____. "Science Education: A Framework for Decision Makers." *Daedalus* 112 (1983): 2.

_____. "Science That Kids Can Live By." *Learning* 2, no. 9 (1974b): 16-21.

_____. *Teaching Science as Continuous Inquiry: A Basic*. 2d ed. New York: McGraw-Hill, 1978.

_____. "Wait Time: Slowing Down May Be a Way of Speeding Up!" *Journal of Teacher Education* 37, no. 1 (1986): 43-50.

Shrum, J. L. "Wait Time and the Use of Target or Native Languages." *Foreign Language Annals* 18 (1985): 4.

Tobin, K. G. "Improving the Quality of Teacher and Student Discourse in Middle School Grades." Paper presented at the annual meeting of the American Educational Research Association, New Orleans, April 1984.

Yeany, R. H., and Porter, C. F. "The Effects of Strategy Analysis on Science Teacher Behaviors: A Meta-Analysis." Paper presented at the annual meeting of the National Association for Research in Science Teaching, Chicago, 1982.

Zdenek, M., and Champion, M. *God Is a Verb*. Waco, Tex.: Word Books, 1974.

6. EFFECTIVE QUESTIONS AND QUESTIONING: A CLASSROOM APPLICATION

by William W. Wilen, Associate Professor of Education, Department of Teacher Development and Curriculum Studies, Kent State University, Ohio

Consultants: Robert J. Stahl, Associate Professor of Secondary Education, Arizona State University, Tempe; and Richard Kindsvatter, Associate Professor of Education, Kent State University, Ohio

The effective teaching research has revealed that a variety of teacher questioning techniques maximize student achievement. The following effective questioning techniques are illustrated within a transcript of a class discussion: question clarity, academic questions, low- and high-level questions, student call-outs, wait time, student response encouragement, volunteer and nonvolunteer balance, correct responses, probing, and acknowledgment and praise. The techniques are analyzed and implications for classroom application are drawn.

Research conducted during the past 20 years has provided useful clues about effective teacher behaviors and techniques that contribute to successful teaching. This is particularly the case in the area of questions and questioning. The research findings related to the kinds of questions teachers ask and the techniques that they use to encourage interaction during recitations and discussions reveal especially effective questioning-related practices.

Effective teaching practices are those teacher behaviors and instructional techniques that research has demonstrated contribute to students' achievement test score gains. Although this is undeniably a limited definition of effective teaching, researchers have focused on this outcome because it is the most pervasive measure of learning. The findings from this body of research are primarily based on correlational studies that revealed relationships between certain teacher behaviors and student achievement. Although positive linkages were made, to assume or claim causality would be inappropriate because valid research investigations of an experimental nature must be conducted. What the research is saying, for example, is that students in classes whose teachers consistently asked clear questions performed better on academic posttests than students in classes whose teachers asked ambiguous questions. Question clarity is one of the positive correlates of student achievement.

The following effective questioning practices have been synthesized from four primary reviews of the effective teaching literature conducted by Brophy and Good (1986), Berliner (1984), Weil and Murphy (1982), and Levin and Long (1981). These reviews were selected because they are comprehensive in their examination of questions and questioning and are relatively recent. While a brief summary of the effective questioning practices is presented here, extended commentary and specific research support for each of the practices were reported by Wilen and Clegg (1986).

Effective teachers:

1. phrase questions clearly;

2. ask questions of primarily an academic nature;

3. ask low-cognitive-level questions (and particularly high frequencies of low-cognitive-level questions with students of low socioeconomic status) in elementary settings;

4. ask high-cognitive-level questions, particularly in intermediate through high school settings;

5. permit student call-outs in low socioeconomic status classes while suppressing call-outs in high socioeconomic status classes, primarily in elementary settings;

6. allow 3 to 5 seconds of wait time after asking a question before requesting a student's response, particularly when high-cognitive-level questions are asked;

7. encourage students to respond in some way to each question asked;

8. balance responses from volunteering and nonvolunteering students;

9. elicit a high percentage of correct responses from students and assist with incorrect responses;

10. probe students' responses to have them clarify ideas, support a point of view, or extend their thinking;

11. acknowledge correct responses from students and use praise specifically and discriminately.

The purpose of this chapter is to illustrate how one might apply these effective questioning practices within a classroom setting. Within this context, teachers might more realistically perceive the potential of how their behaviors and techniques can affect student learning. The effective teaching research has been conducted in classes representing a wide range of grade levels and subject areas but the conclusions reached are strongest for basic skills instruction in the primary grades. While some of the questioning techniques have been found to be particularly effective at the elementary level, there are obvious implications for the application of all eleven of the effective questioning techniques at the secondary level. Research has shown that clearly expressed higher-level questions, wait time, and probing techniques are more evident and effective within a discussion format in classes at the secondary level. A simulated high school class discussion was designed to demonstrate, relatively realistically and specifically, all eleven effective questioning practices, with accompanying student reactions. A transcript of a hypothetical twelfth grade sociology class is presented and accompanied with marginal explanatory notes keyed to the eleven effective questioning practices. The topic of sex equity and discrimination was selected because it is a critical problem evident in our society that is reflected on and discussed in many social studies classes. Commentary related to each of the practices follows and implications for classroom application are drawn.

TRANSCRIPT

T1: For the past week we have been studying issues related to sex equity and particularly how women have been discriminated against historically. We have looked at what individuals and organizations have done to try to bring about change. I would like to turn from the political aspects of discrimination to the more economic and social ones. I think in this way we will be able to see more realistically how and why this conflict of values exists between men and women.

Before I forget, I want to let you know how much I really appreciated how conscientiously you completed the readings and preparation for class. This was very obvious to me in the quality of the questions you asked when our guest speaker was here. She was an interesting speaker and you were a fine audience.

Today we'll begin examining discrimination from a more social perspective. Let's start with examining the extent sex equity exists in the home situation. We're going to become a little more personal with what we share in our discussions. As in the past, I want you to feel free to contribute your experiences and opinions. Remember also that you have the right to privacy. Today our objective is to evaluate the role of women as housewives in terms of their responsibilities as people generally perceive them. Are they being discriminated against? This will get us ready for tomorrow when you share your plans as to how two partners can share equitably their responsibilities. I think we will learn a lot from each other.

Rhetorical question

T2: WHO HAS READ A JOB WANT AD RECENTLY? (several students raise their hands)

Procedural lesson entry question

T3: Aaron, WHAT WAS THE POSITION ADVERTISED IN THE AD YOU READ?

Knowledge-level question

S1: A lumberyard assistant

Knowledge-level response

T4: WHAT DID THE AD SAY?

Knowledge-level probe for elaboration

110

S2: Carter Lumber needs two warehouse stock assistants for the summer. I think the position pays $4.00 per hour. Hope I get the position because I applied for it. Man, could I use the money!

Knowledge-level response

T5: Thanks, Aaron. ANY OTHERS CARE TO TELL US ABOUT THE ADS YOU HAVE READ LATELY? (two other students describe their ads)

Provides encouragment/ redirects question to two other students

T6: I'd like you to read this want ad and share your impressions. (passes out the following ad) ANYONE NOT GET A COPY? (students read individually)

Procedural question

> WANTED: Woman who can help in house and home 18-hour day, 7-day week. Sleep in. No wages. No social security or retirement benefits. Coffee breaks occasionally. Modest clothes allowance. Must have working knowledge of marketing, cooking, sewing, medicine, education, psychology, elementary electricity and plumbing, gardening, entertaining, and bookkeeping. Driver's license required. Position suitable for one more interested in steady employment than in advancement. One who can work part time for extra money preferred. (Miller and Johson 1976)

S3: (calls out): Is the ad for real?

Contributing call-out/ student-initiated question

T7: No, it's fictional. WHAT'S YOUR REACTION? (several students raise their hands) (pauses 4 seconds) John?

Teacher responds/ broad affectively oriented evaluation-level question/wait time 1 (post question)

S4: It looks like someone is advertising for a mother.

Analysis-level response

T8: I don't think taking care of children was mentioned.

Assists student with inaccurate response

S5: I mean housewife.

Continued response

111

T9: (followup to John's response): Okay. DO YOU THINK THE JOB DESCRIPTION IS ACCURATE?	Acknowledgement/ evaluation-level probe to extend thinking
S6: I guess, although in our house my mother also seems to have time doing some fun things like watching TV and visiting friends. But, she is also looking for a part-time job to bring in some extra money. I'm not sure how she can do it all.	Evaluation-level response with support
T10: WHAT DO THE REST OF YOU THINK? Jeremy? (hand raised)	Redirects question
S7: My parents both work full time and we all share the work.	Student responds at different (knowledge) level
T11: (Nods head to Claire who has her hand raised)	Redirects question
S8: It seems accurate to me. At first I thought it was for a housekeeper but then I saw no salary was involved. I never realized that a wife has so many responsibilities.	Evaluation-level response with support
T12: (followup to Claire's response): Yes. WHAT SPECIFIC SKILLS ARE INVOLVED IN, FOR EXAMPLE, THE BOOKKEEPING RESPONSIBILITY?	Acknowledgement/ knowledge-level probe for elaboration
S9: Keeping a balanced budget, or at least making sure that there is enough money to pay the bills. Writing checks and making bank deposits and withdrawals ...	Knowledge-level response
S10: (calls out): Keeping track of life and home insurance.	Contributing call-out/ knowledge-level response
T13: Right. IN ORDER TO APPLY FOR THIS POSITION, HOW MUCH EDUCATION SHOULD A WOMAN HAVE? (2-second pause) Andrew? (hand raised)	Acknowledgment/ evaluation-level question/wait time 1

S11: She should probably have at least a college degree to do all that is necessary. (students laugh) Just kidding. I think she needs a high school education.

Evaluation-level response without support

S12: (call-out): I don't agree. My mother didn't even finish 9th grade when she got married!

Contributing call-out/ evaluation-level response without support/ student-student interaction

T14: (followup to previous response): HOW DID SHE LEARN ALL THAT WAS NEEDED TO BE A HOUSE-WIFE AND MOTHER?

Analysis-level probe to provide support for point of view

S13: I guess she just learned from her mother, and talking to friends and neighbors. She learned by doing, not from a school education.

Analysis-level response

T15: It sounds like she learned from others' experiences. That's how most of us learned to be mothers. Suppose the ad was for real. DO YOU BELIEVE A WOMAN WHO ACCEPTED THE POSITION WOULD BE EXPLOITED? (5-second pause) Jeremy? (hand raised)

Evaluation-level question/wait time 1

S14: You know, I was thinking that. After all, she is not receiving a salary, only room and board for 18 hours a day work, seven days a week. That's exploitation in my book! Could even be called slavery.

Evaluation-level response with support

S15: (calls out): But she doesn't have to accept the position. It can't be exploitation if she has the freedom of choice. She can even quit if the job is not to her liking. Slaves did not have that option.

Contributing call-out/ evaluation-level response with support/ student-student interaction

S16: (calls out): But, that's just the point, Andrew! Housewives don't have the freedom of choice; they can't just quit! Divorce isn't even a real option for many women. Women are stuck in the home and are being exploited, and many don't even realize it.

Another contributing call-out/evaluation-level response with support/ student-student interaction continued

113

T16: You've made some excellent points! The want ad is fictional but the responsibilities that a homemaker has as described here are pretty accurate. The only major difference is that the number of traditional homemakers is decreasing. More women are working full time, many in careers. Also, more women are expecting, and demanding, that the work in the home be shared. (pause) Let me change the want ad slightly. SUPPOSE THE AD WAS FOR A MAN?

Praise

Ambiguous question

S17: (calls out): What do you mean?

Contributing call-out/ student question for purpose of clarification

T17: We've been examining the role of a housewife. Let's think about a househusband. HOW REALISTIC IS IT FOR A MAN TO ASSUME THESE RESPONSIBILITIES IN THE HOME? (5-second pause) Eric? (hand raised)

Rephrased evaluation-level question/ wait time 1

S18: First of all, this is not the type of work traditionally done by men. Men are conditioned to be the major provider for a family and therefore need a salary—the higher the better.

Evaluation-level response

T18: Uh huh ... (3-second pause)

Encouragement/wait time 2 (post response)

S19: (continuing) I mean ... the position has traditionally been filled by women in the home. Call them what you like—housewives, homemakers, slaves—it doesn't matter. Somebody needs to do the work and take responsibility for managing the home and raising the children. Women have traditionally fulfilled this role and more than likely will continue to do so for a long time.

Evaluation-level response continued with support

T19: WHAT DO YOU THINK, MIKE?

Redirects evaluation-level question to a nonvolunteer

S20: (silence—3 seconds)

Wait time 1

114

T20: TO WHAT EXTENT SHOULD A MAN ASSUME THESE RESPONSIBILITIES IN THE HOME?	Rephrases question
S21: (continued silence—2 seconds)	Wait time 1
T21: You look tired. ARE YOU FEELING OKAY? SUPPOSE I COME BACK TO YOU LATER?	Combination of affective and procedural questions
S22: Okay.	
T22: Leslie, you look like you have something to say.	Redirects evaluation question to another nonvolunteer
S23: I know it is hard to imagine a man doing this work but the idea of a househusband is not unusual to me. My parents know a couple who reversed roles completely. She has a career and, because he was laid off from his job two years ago, he manages the home. As far as I know he's not planning to go back to a full-time job. He's happy at home.	Comprehension-level response
T23: An interesting situation. I think it would be valuable to have him, or some other male in a similar situation speak to the class. Well, most of you seem to agree that many women are being taken advantage of in their traditional role as homemakers. HOW WOULD YOU CHANGE THE LAWS ... WHAT LAWS CAN WE ADVISE THE NATIONAL ORGANIZATION FOR WOMEN TO LOBBY FOR TO PROTECT HOME-MAKERS? (4-second pause) Emily? (hand raised)	Encouragement/run-on synthesis-level question/ wait time 1
S24: I'm glad you asked that one! I have to spend a lot of time at home helping raise my younger brothers because my mother is a single parent and, of course, works full time. I think we should propose that homemakers should be paid a minimum wage by the spouse working outside the home and be given benefits such as retirement. She should also have time off away from the home, perhaps two or three nights each week. Maybe more!	Synthesis-level response

T24: You obviously feel pretty strongly about that, Emily. Anna? (hand raised)

Encouragement / redirects question

S25: I think that marriages should be arranged by contract with both husband and wife agreeing to terms. That will cut out, or at least reduce the possibility of, exploitation.

Synthesis-level response

T25: WHAT DO YOU MEAN BY A CONTRACT?

Knowledge-level probe for clarification

S26: I mean a signed agreement worked out by a lawyer.

Knowledge-level response

T26: The contract approach could also be used by those men and women who have decided to live together before getting married. (pause) You know, I can't imagine any of my friends ever applying for the position in the want ad under any circumstances. (many students raise their hands) (3-second pause) John?

Declarative statement / wait time 1

S27: I would spend my life on skid row before taking that job.

Evaluation-level response without support

T27: (followup to John's response): THEN HOW WOULD YOU REACT IF YOUR FUTURE WIFE SAID SHE IS HAVING SECOND THOUGHTS ABOUT MAR-RYING YOU IF THIS IS WHAT YOU ARE EXPECTING FROM A HOMEMAKER?

Affectively oriented evaluation-level probe to provide support for point of view

S28: (continuing) I think that would be a little different. More than likely we would probably have to agree to some kind of shared role. I see the point you are getting at. . . . But, I still would not take the job because it is too much for one person.

Continued evaluation-level response with support

T28: YOUR THOUGHTS, CLAIRE?

Redirects to a nonvolunteer

116

S29: I would take it only if the economy was in bad shape—like during a severe recession. I would also only take it on a temporary basis, perhaps even part time. Would you take the position?

Evaluation-level response with support

Student-initiated question

T29: No, I can't imagine any circumstances in which I would take it. But I don't know what I would do if the bottom dropped out of the economy and I had no job for several years. (pause) Thanks for being so open and offering your opinions.

Encouragement

Since the class period has been shortened by the assembly, I would like you to think about what we have been discussing and take a couple of minutes to write down one question you would like to have answered about sex equity in the home. (3-minute pause—students write questions)

Written student questions

For your assignment this evening, I would like you to write a want ad for your future wife or husband, assuming you plan to marry, of course. Design a want ad that you would be willing to share either with the class or me.

Synthesis-level assignment

I think we had an excellent discussion today because some interesting perspectives were revealed about sex equity. I am looking forward to tomorrow's class. See you. Mike, could I see you for a minute, please.

117

DISCUSSION

Clear Questions

Effective teachers phrase questions clearly. Questions are interrogative sentences that communicate content and direction to the students, and function as instructional cues intended to stimulate thought and speech. A student who responds reflectively to a question engages in the process of hearing, deciphering, considering information pertinent to the question, forming a response, expressing it orally, and perhaps revising it, depending on the teacher's reaction (Gall 1984). If students are miscued by an ambiguous question, the probability of confusion is increased. If this practice occurs often, frustration, withdrawal, and resentment develop. Clearly phrased questions communicate to the students precisely the response expectation.

Poorly phrased and run-on questions are major sources of ambiguity, especially in discussions. Vague questions force students to try to guess what the teacher wants rather than to use the time more productively to think of a response. Run-on questions are two or more uninterrupted, sometimes incomplete, questions in a series. Frustration occurs as students attempt to guess which question to answer.

Questions also trigger different levels of thought. Ideally, the cognitive level of the student's response is congruent to the level of thinking intended by the teacher's question. In reality, there is only about a 50 percent correlation between the cognitive levels of teachers' questions and students' responses (Mills et al. 1980) This also can lead to confusion and frustration.

In the above illustrative discussion, most of the teacher's questions were appropriately responded to by the students as noticed in the content of their responses and by their lack of expressed confusion. At one point an ambiguous question was asked ("Suppose the ad was for a man?" T16). A student immediately, and appropriately reacted with "What do you mean?" (S17). Once the question was rephrased with more clarity and appropriate cues, it was answered and the discussion continued. At another point, the teacher started a run-on sentence (T23) and then rephrased it to eliminate the confusion.

For the most part, the thought levels of students' responses were congruent with the teacher's questions. In the entry to the lesson, a broad, open-ended question (T7) was posed to invite student consideration of its content. Analysis (S4-S5) and evaluation-level (S8) responses

118

were provided except in one case, in which a student commented at the knowledge level (S7). A similar situation occurred later in the discussion. At that time a student volunteered a personal experience at the comprehension-level (S23) in response to an evaluation-level question.

One implication for teaching is that key higher-cognitive-level questions need to be planned prior to class, perhaps in written form, in order that appropriate student responses can be obtained. Another implication is that teachers may need to acquaint, and perhaps train, their students in the different levels of questions and responses in order to increase the probability that clear communications will occur. The use of verbal cues is another way of communicating a teacher's intention to students regarding the level of thinking desired. The research suggests that clearly phrased questions lead to higher student involvement, a greater correct response rate and higher academic achievement.

Academic Questions

Effective teachers ask questions of primarily an academic nature. Academic questions are those that relate to the subject matter or content taught. These questions focus on the facts, concepts, generalizations, skills, attitudes, and values that generally constitute the content of subjects at the elementary and secondary levels. Nonacademic questions are those that are generally affectively or procedurally oriented. Sometimes teachers will use affective questions to show acceptance of students' feelings and to demonstrate empathy for students or toward a particular situation. Because they contribute to the social-emotional climate, these questions can play an important role in any classroom. In positive climate settings, students feel more free, relaxed, secure, and are more willing to become more mentally involved and more active participants.

Teachers can use clear, precise procedural questions to manage the daily operation of the classroom and to direct students' behavior. They should most often be used at the beginning and end of the class period and when instructional shifts occur and assignments are explained. The most recent estimate of the time teachers spend asking procedural and affective questions is 20 percent. The remaining 80 percent is devoted to academic questions (Gall 1970).

In the illustration lesson, the teacher primarily used academically oriented questions to guide student thinking during the lesson. Most of

119

the questions related to the fictitious ad illustrating the problems of housewives. On several occasions the teacher used procedural and affective questions that facilitated and encouraged communication. The discussion was initiated with a procedural question (T2) that helped focus students' attention. Then, while copies of the ad were being passed out, the teacher asked another form of a procedural question (T6) to find out whether all students had received a copy. In the situation with Mike, the nonresponsive student, the teacher reacted to his apparent fatigued look with a question suggesting personal concern for his health (T21)—"Are you feeling okay?" The question was almost rhetorically stated because an empathetic procedural question immediately followed. The teacher intended to show interest in ascertaining Mike's thought about the topic but also to move the discussion along by involving other students.

The implication for teaching is that lessons should be more structured to increase the probability that academically oriented environments are created. The degree to which academic content is emphasized depends in large part on the objectives for the lesson and the kinds of questions asked. Although procedural and affective questions are necessary and important in many situations, they should not become a focus if gain in student achievement is an important consideration.

Low-Level Questions

Effective teachers ask low-cognitive-level questions, and particularly, high frequencies of low-cognitive-level questions with students of low socioeconomic status, in elementary settings. Low-cognitive-level questions correspond to Bloom's (1956) knowledge level where the emphasis is on recalling facts and information. Approximately 75 percent of the cognitive questions teachers ask are at the knowledge level (Gall 1970; Hare and Pulliam 1980). A high frequency of this type of question is characteristic of recitations for which the teacher's purpose is that students review subject matter.

Recitation is an important method in the teacher's instructional repertoire because of its demonstrated effectiveness in determining the extent students know the essential facts. Clear and focused recitation is effective because of the practice students get with the subject matter shortly after reading, viewing, or listening to it. Repetition coupled with immediate feedback is a proven combination in strengthening students' cognitive recall skills (Gall 1984). The major criticism of teachers' disproportionate use of low-cognitive-level questions is that recall tends to become an end in itself rather than serving to stimulate higher-level thinking about an issue or problem.

The demonstration teacher engaged students in a discussion rather than a recitation and at the high school level rather than the elementary level. As such, the focus was on asking higher-cognitive-level questions, not those that could be classified as knowledge level. Only one knowledge-level question was asked to initiate a discussion phase while several were asked as followup probing questions for the purpose of clarification and elaboration. In the entry to the discussion, the teacher asked Aaron the name of the position he had read in the want ads (T3). Aaron's response (S1) was then probed for an elaboration of the ad (T4), which resulted in knowledge-level thinking (S2). On two other occasions the teacher used followup probing questions to request that students provide additional information (T12, T25). Both probing questions and student responses were at the knowledge level.

Most of the research that supports the finding that higher frequencies of low-cognitive-level questions lead to higher achievement was conducted in urban settings with disadvantaged urban children in the basic skill areas of mathematics and reading. The implication, especially for elementary teachers, is that precise and clear knowledge-level questions facilitate learning of the basic skills and facts. As such they are a useful means to diagnose and test students' recall of basic facts. An implication for teachers at all levels is that recitations can be an effective means to allow students to practice recalling the subject matter information they are to recall later.

High-Level Questions

Effective teachers ask high-cognitive-level questions, particularly in intermediate through high school settings. High-cognitive-level teacher questions stimulate students' thinking in the five levels above the knowledge level: comprehension, application, analysis, synthesis, and evaluation (Bloom 1956). At these levels, students engage in a wide range of cognitive activities, from interpreting and comparing information to hypothesizing solutions and assessing points of view. Only about 25 percent of the cognitive questions the typical teachers ask are likely to be at these levels (Gall 1970; Hare and Pulliam 1980). High-cognitive questions are an essential characteristic of discussions in the classroom during which the teacher and students use information they have as they explore topics, issues, and problems.

Although nearly all sessions involving interaction between the teacher and students in classrooms are labeled discussion, in reality most are recitations with a sprinkling of higher-level questions. In addition to the inclusion of more higher-cognitive-level questions, discussion must feature more student-talk than teacher-talk and considerable student-student interaction. The teacher's task is that of facilitator, in contrast to the tester role that is characteristic of recitation. Effective reflective inquiry strategies use the discussion method as the primary means to stimulate student interest in and exploration of a problem or issue.

Of the six primary academic questions asked by the demonstration teacher (T3, T7, T13, T15, T16-17, T23), five could be classified as higher-cognitive questions at the synthesis and evaluation levels. This count does not include the redirected and probing questions employed as followups to the main questions, most of which fit the evaluation level. With the fictitious job ad serving as the springboard, the teacher's objective in this lesson was for the students to judge the responsibilities women have in the home to determine if they are being discriminated against. This evaluation-level objective is achieved by the emphasis on evaluation-level questions asked by the teacher during the discussion. After the students read the fictitious ad, the teacher followed immediately with an open-ended, affectively oriented evaluation-level question (T7) to get students on task, thinking, and involved. The label "affectively oriented" was applied to this evaluation-level question because students' feelings and attitudes seem to be called upon in order to respond. Questions at the higher-cognitive levels tend to stimulate responses in the affective domain. After several redirects and probes, an evaluation question related to a housewife's level of education followed (T13). Discussion followed on exploitation and role reversals prompted by two other evaluation-level questions (T15, T16-17). The teacher then challenged students with a synthesis-level question to consider how the discrimination problem might be solved (T23). Additional evidence indicating a discussion rather than a recitation had occurred is student-student interaction and the predominance of student talk. Approximately 60 percent of the verbalizations can be attributed to the students in the illustrative lesson if the focus is on the discussion excluding the teacher's entry and closure.

The research supporting the positive relationship between higher-level questions and students' achievement gains was conducted primarily at the middle and secondary school levels. One implication for teaching is that if teachers expect to increase the probability that their students will engage in higher-level thinking, questions must be planned at cognitive levels above knowledge. Although developing students' ability to think reflectively at the higher levels is a goal of most subjects, many classes nevertheless tend to be characterized by recitation and consequently low-level thinking.

Student Call-Outs

Effective teachers permit student call-outs in low-socioeconomic-status classes while supressing call-outs in high-socioeconomic-status classes, primarily in elementary settings. Students calling-out an answer to a question during a recitation or an opinion during a discussion may be received enthusiastically by some teachers but may be threatening to others. The difference in perception lies in the complexity of the teaching situation. Possible variables that enter into the decision to establish a more unstructured and open environment include the maturity, inherent motivation level, and ability levels of the students; number of students and class behavior patterns; nature of the subject matter being presented; and the teacher's personality. Call-outs can be very useful in encouraging low-ability, reticent students to get involved. In classes containing high-ability, assertive and confident students, their eagerness to respond may need to be more restrained.

In the example lesson, which was conducted in a high school setting, the demonstration teacher's students were average to above average in ability. In addition, judging from the lack of control problems and acceptance of students' verbal contributions, their general conduct was acceptable to the teacher. The demonstration teacher encouraged students to raise their hands if they wanted to respond to a question or make a comment but, at the same time, permitted students to call-out their responses. This apparent violation of the effective questioning principle seemed to be necessitated by the teacher's need for a less structured, more open interaction to achieve the objective of the lesson. The first call-out (S3) was from a student who had read the ad and wanted to know if it was real. The teacher responded and moved toward interaction with the rest of the class, suggesting that the call-out was not premature. The next call-out (S10) came from a student who added

123

factual information to another student's response. The third call-out (S12) offered a differing point of view. Extended student-student interaction occurred as two students contributed their opinions on exploitation (S15, S16). The teacher was obviously quite pleased with their call-out contributions as indicated in the reaction, "You've made some excellent points." Only one other call-out occurred, that in the form of a question requesting clarification for an ambiguous question (S17). All call-outs were positive contributions to the discussion and they were accepted by the teacher.

The research relating questioning techniques to students' gains in achievement supports call-outs in classes with students who are not active participants. This is particularly the case in urban classrooms containing poorer children. The implication for teaching is that reticent students can make positive contributions to recitations and discussions through their call-outs and should be encouraged to do so as long as they contribute in a responsible and positive way. Call-outs to higher-level questions may need to be managed in classes with more impulsive and/or assertive students. Teachers ultimately need to decide the degree of structure that is necessary for effective use of recitation and discussion in order to achieve lesson objectives. This structure will be a major factor in determining the extent call-outs are encouraged or discouraged.

Wait Time

Effective teachers allow 3 to 5 seconds of wait time after asking a question before requesting a student's response, particularly when high-cognitive questions are asked. Wait time is one of the most essential techniques used in questioning because of its demonstrated impact on the interaction between a teacher and students. The teacher's deliberate use of 3- to 5-second pauses during a discussion can occur at two different yet critical points in the dialog. Wait time 1 (post question wait time) is a deliberate, uninterrupted pause after a teacher asks a question prior to the initiation of a student's response. Wait time 2 (post response wait time) is an identical pause after a student responds before the teacher reacts or another student responds. Research has shown that the typical teacher pauses approximately 1 second after asking a question before calling on a student and 1 second after a student has responded before probing the response, redirecting the question to another student, rephrasing the question, or answering the original question (Rowe 1974). Although wait time has a use during recitations, it is vitally important and effective during discussions geared toward inducing higher-level thinking.

Teachers have been successfully trained to increase their use of wait time during discussions in the classroom. One of the most recent studies found that as teachers increased their pauses to 3 seconds, the quantity and quality of students' responses increased significantly. Teachers' use of wait time caused more students to respond, to give longer responses, and to ask a greater number of higher-cognitive-level questions (Swift and Gooding 1983). An extensive review of the impact teachers have in using wait time in the classroom can be found in Chapter 5 of this book.

The demonstration teacher purposely used wait time 1 every time a primary question was asked and wait time 2 in one instance. Five primary questions were asked at the synthesis and evaluation levels (T7, T13, T15, T16-17, T23). The length of the pauses ranged from 2 to 5 seconds. On one occasion, the teacher used 3 seconds of wait time when a question was redirected to Mike (T19). After rephrasing the question, another 2-second pause was used, although unsuccessfully, to stimulate participation. In this case, it is difficult to determine whether additional wait time would have stimulated Mike to respond. Immediately preceding the encounter with Mike the teacher effectively used wait time 2 to encourage an extension of thinking (T18). Eric initially responded to an evaluation-level question. Then the teacher responded with mild encouragement ("Uh huh") followed by 3 seconds more of wait time. The student continued with a more lengthy and reflective response. Without this second use of wait time, further thinking and extended expression by Eric probably would not have occurred.

Teachers who use wait time consistently as a questioning technique increase the probability of their students' achievement gains. Many teachers rely heavily on recitations and discussions to achieve objectives. The implication is that teachers need to pause conscientiously after asking questions and after students respond in order to increase the frequency and improve the quality of students' responses.

Encouraging Student Response

Effective teachers encourage students to respond in some way to each question asked. Encouraging students to respond in some way to every question asked establishes very clearly the expectation that the teacher is seeking and desires active student participation. There is a positive relationship between the percentage of questions answered by students and their achievement. This expectation of response should apply to students volunteering to answer teacher questions as well as to nonvolunteering students called upon to contribute. If, for example, a nonvolunteering student does not know the answer, or does not care to express an opinion related to an issue being discussed, the student should still be expected to utter something that indicates he or she heard the question. Even an "I don't know" response can be an acceptable minimal response.

Redirection can be used to stimulate thought and a response to an unanswered question. Although the research on the use of redirection in relation to gains in student achievement is mixed, it has been shown to be a useful technique to encourage participation. Questions can be redirected to volunteering and nonvolunteering students.

Regarding the demonstration teacher's performance, at least one student responded to each of the six primary questions asked. Further, each response to the six questions was followed by a teacher probe and/or the question was redirected to other students. At one point (T15), considerable student-student interaction occurred when two students called-out their opinions in reaction to Jeremy who initially responded to the teacher's question.

Redirection was used extensively, a technique that would be appropriate in a discussion focusing on a controversial issue such as sex discrimination. The teacher redirected three questions (T3, T7, T16-17) two times each. On one occasion (T19) the teacher experienced some frustration in getting Mike, a nonvolunteering student, to respond to a question that was redirected to him. Finally, after rephrasing the question, use of wait time on two occasions, and after a combination of affective and procedural questions (T21), he responded with an "Okay." The teacher indirectly communicated the intent to the class that students had to respond in some way to each question asked. Most teachers would not have persevered to this extent.

The implication for teaching is that expectations need to be communicated to the students to increase the probability that discussions will achieve the objectives established for the lesson. One of those expectations should be that students must participate in the interaction and that all questions need to be answered in some way. Another implication is that the more questions that are answered, the probability of higher student achievement is increased.

Volunteers and Nonvolunteers

Effective teachers balance responses from volunteering and nonvolunteering students. Students gain in achievement in classrooms where the teacher has purposely balanced volunteering students' interactive contributions with those of nonvolunteers. When there is a high probability that nonvolunteers know the answer or have a contribution, they need to be encouraged to participate.

However, in most classrooms the scene that occurs is that of a small group of students who willingly and consistently contribute their reactions and ideas during whole-class discussions. Also apparent is the large number of students who have decided not to participate orally and, in many cases, mentally. Although not to the degree noticed in discussions, this phenomenon is also evident during recitations. The purpose of a recitation is to review previously considered information during which the majority of students are expected to demonstrate knowledge of the topic.

One approach to involve nonvolunteers is to encourage student-student interaction, particularly during discussions. During such interaction, not only are more students involved in offering ideas, perspectives and judgments, they are more active participants in and assume more responsibility for their own learning. In a recent research study (Wood and Wood 1987), it was found that teachers exert considerable control in discussions through their questions. As a result, students' freedom to participate is often stifled because they have become dependent on the teacher. Encouraging student-student interaction by involving a balance of volunteering and nonvolunteering students forces the focus to shift from the teacher to the students. The discussion process thereby contributes to students' "ownership" of the learning activity.

The demonstration teacher stimulated considerable interaction during the discussion with a balance of contributions from volunteering and nonvolunteering students. Volunteering students participated by having their raised hands acknowledged by the teacher in response to a question or by calling-out responses. Three nonvolunteering students participated, two substantially (S23, S29) and one (S20-22), very minimally. The situation with Mike (T19), the nonresponsive student, has been described previously. Immediately following the teacher's attempt to involve him, the question was redirected to another nonvolunteer (T22), Leslie, who contributed an interesting experience relevant to the issue. Toward the end of the discussion, Claire was called on (T28). She provided a realistic point of view and also initiated a question (S29). Significantly, the responses from the nonvolunteering students were important in keeping the discussion going and achieving the objective of the lesson.

The implication is that teachers may underestimate the potential contributions of nonvolunteering students during discussions. Balancing the participation of volunteering and nonvolunteering students can increase verbal and mental involvement, stimulate more student-student interaction and, as research has demonstrated, increase the probability of students' achievement.

Correct Responses from Students

Effective teachers elicit a high percentage of correct responses from students and assist with incorrect responses. This questioning technique applies primarily to recitations during which the teacher emphasizes students' recall of facts. The assumption is that the students have had access to the answers prior to the recitation, usually by reading the book, text, or handout, viewing a demonstration, film or other media, or listening to a reading or presentation. An emphasis on knowledge-level thinking results in the habitual use of memorized information to answer teacher questions.

A teacher can increase the probability of obtaining a high percentage of "right" answers by preparing students for the recitation through such learning tasks as in-class activities, homework assignments, or evaluation exercises. When incorrect responses are verbalized, the teacher should rephrase the question or give more specific clues. An important consideration during this corrective feedback process is to create a supportive social-emotional climate within which students are encouraged to participate. The use of wait time can also encourage students to maintain focus. However, overuse of wait time can slow the pace and, perhaps, defeat the purpose of recitation as an instructional method.

The example lesson demonstrated a discussion rather than a recitation. As such, the emphasis was on students' projecting ideas and opinions at the higher-cognitive levels rather than merely recalling relevant data. Only one knowledge-level question was asked and this occurred at the beginning of the lesson. Only on one occasion (T8) did the teacher assist a student with a response. The teacher asked for a reaction to the want ad. John responded inaccurately and the teacher invited rethinking with a followup statement. In this indirect way, the

128

teacher assisted the student to produce a "correct" response.

The implication for teaching is that the effectiveness of recitations is dependent on how well the students are prepared for the question-answer session and how incorrect responses are then handled by the teacher. If a high percentage of correct responses characterizes the recitation and the teacher has assisted students with incorrect responses in a supportive manner, the probability is high that students' achievement will be affected positively.

Probing

Effective teachers probe students' responses to have them clarify the response, to support a point of view, or to extend their thinking. The technique of probing is particularly evident during discussions when students' responses are more complex than they are during recitations. This complexity reflects higher-level thinking, particularly at the analysis, synthesis, and evaluation levels. Often students lack the experience of thinking and expressing themselves at the higher cognitive levels. The result is that responses may be ambiguous, incomplete, or superficial. This occurs particularly in classrooms where the primary emphasis has been on recall of relevant information with only minimal attention given to helping students think about this information. The technique of probing can make the difference between discussions that are "bull sessions" and those that are reflective inquiry experiences.

When implemented by teachers in a supportive manner, probing is an effective technique. Typically, during discussions, probing encourages students to complete or clarify a response by adding more information or rephrasing what has previously been said. It is also used to extend thinking by having students provide support for a given point of view or judgment. Further, when used effectively, probes elevate thinking to higher cognitive levels. A critical factor in its effectiveness is that probes must be used in a supportive, inviting manner during interaction in order to avoid placing students in threatening or intimidating situations.

The demonstration teacher probed initial student responses to questions on six occasions. Three probes were used for the purpose of having students clarify and elaborate their responses, and three probes invited students to extend their thinking. The three elaboration probes (T4, T25, T12) followed responses to knowledge, synthesis, and evaluation-level questions. The students' followup responses to these probes were at

129

the knowledge level (S2, S26, S9). This pattern of response reflects the typical situation in which probes are used for clarification or elaboration. Regarding the probes to extend thinking, the three probes (T9, T27, T14) followed responses to two evaluation questions and one declarative statement. Two of the students' followup responses to the probes (S13, S28) provided support for their points of view and the other (S6) was an indication of additional thought. In these cases, the probes worked to extend student thinking, as evidenced by the content of their responses to these probes.

The implication for teaching is that students will respond more completely and reflectively to questions, particularly at the higher cognitive levels characteristic of discussion, when probes are used. If teachers use probes effectively to help students clarify, elaborate, extend and support their responses, the probability that their students' achievement will be enhanced is increased.

Acknowledgment and Praise

Effective teachers acknowledge correct responses from students and are specific and discriminating in their use of praise. Although not strictly considered questioning techniques, acknowledgment and praise are important means to encourage students to participate within recitations and discussions. Acknowledgment is simply a verbal or nonverbal behavior communicating the rightness or wrongness, or acceptance or rejection, of a student's response to a question. This form of encouragement is more likely to be found in recitations than in discussions because of the focus on right answers. Praise is an indicator to the student of a teacher's value judgment of the response. When certain praise behaviors sometimes are overused by teachers, they then lack credibility and effect. This results in these behaviors not serving the purpose for which they were intended, that is, to reinforce and reward students for their verbal contributions to the interaction. Simple acknowledgments and other forms of encouragement often can be used in place of praise to communicate acceptance to students of their verbal contributions.

Praise is most effective when it is used discriminately and specifically. Discriminate use occurs when the teacher informs a student that a response is exceptional or outstanding. The most powerful pattern of praise behavior is that which communicates both praise and the reason for the praise. This intentional, appropriate use of rewards seems to have the most potential in terms of influencing students' attitudes and behaviors during recitations and discussions.

The teacher in the example balanced the use of acknowledgment and praise behaviors. In addition, a variety of indirect verbalizations was used to encourage students to participate in the discussion. Acknowledgment, in the form of "yes," "right," and "okay," was used on three occasions following student responses (S8, S9-10, S5). Praise was used very discriminately only once after a major student-student interactive phase involving three students (S14, S15, S16): "You've made some excellent points." An evaluation-level question (T15) stimulated this interaction. Praise was also used on two other occasions as a means to help establish a supportive social-emotional climate. In the introduction to the lesson (T1), the teacher praised the students for their conscientious preparation for a guest speaker and for being a "fine audience." Also, in the closure (T29), the teacher commented that the discussion was "excellent" and that she/he was "looking forward to tomorrow's class." In both the entry and closure, praise was followed by specific reasons for the praise.

The teacher also used statements of encouragement that indirectly communicated acceptance of and appreciation for students' responses to primary and redirected questions. "Thanks" was expressed after a student's response (S1-2) to a question early in the discussion (T5) and in the closure (T29), the teacher expressed thanks to the students for being open and expressing opinions. On several other occasions the teacher showed acceptance of students' ideas (T15, T23), and acceptance of another student's feelings (T24). When used appropriately over time, these forms of encouragement are likely to contribute to developing and maintaining a positive climate during discussions.

The implication is that teachers need to directly encourage students' contributions during both recitations and discussions by using acknowledgment and praise. Further, the teacher must be judicious, specific, and witting in the use of praise. According to research, the result will be the increased participation of students and possible gains in their academic achievement.

CONCLUSION

This chapter focused on eleven questioning-related practices that, when used appropriately, correlate positively with gains in student achievement. It illustrated how these effective questioning practices might be applied in a high school classroom setting. Although much research is needed to determine the degree of their respective impacts, their thrust is clearly evident. Investigation is also needed on other practices that have demonstrated effectiveness in stimulating interaction within recitation and discussion settings. The influence of these alternative approaches on student achievement needs to be clarified. Two in particular are of current interest in the literature on questioning—student-initiated questions and nonquestion alternatives, such as the use of declarative statements.

A teacher's encouragement of student-initiated questions during discussions, for example, has the potential to shift more control of the discussion and responsibility for significant, on-task thinking to students. The outcome is that students may begin to assume more direction for their own learning (Hunkins 1985). An illustration of how this might be accomplished can be noticed in the transcript. As a followup to the discussion (T29), the teacher had the students write one question they would like to have answered about sex equity. The inference is that the questions, along with the want ads to be designed for homework, would be the basis for continuing the discussion the next day. Chapter 8 of this book further discusses the role student questions can play in the classroom.

The use of nonquestion alternatives to stimulate students' thinking and participation in discussions and recitation is also worthy of continued research study. Some of these alternatives are a teacher's use of statements instead of questions, restating students' ideas, inviting elaboration, and two others that have been discussed previously—wait time and student-initiated questions (Dillon 1983). Research suggests that use of these alternatives, particularly declarative statements, tend to produce a greater quantity and quality of discussion (Dillon 1984). Some of these alternative approaches are noticed in the transcript. The most obvious one is the extensive and purposeful use of wait time to encourage greater student mental and verbal involvement in the discussion. On one other occasion (T26), the teacher made a declarative statement about a personal observation related to the want ad instead of asking a question. This resulted in several evaluation-level student responses and a student question directed to the teacher. Although the influence of nonquestion alternatives and student-initiated questions on students' achievement gains has not been determined, their use in conjunction with questioning can offer teachers an expanded repertoire

132

of techniques to stimulate interaction in the classroom. Chapter 3 of this book provides a rationale for the use of nonquestion alternatives in discussions.

As a result of being charged with the responsibility of preparing reflective, caring, and active citizens, one may readily idealize social studies teachers involving their students in discussions about current critical issues through their skillful use of questions and other interactive techniques. The reality is that many teachers, representing all the subject areas, are generally unfamiliar with the diversity of questioning levels and techniques that are essential to conducting meaningful discussions. Teachers are even less familiar with the impact their questions have on students' achievement. The implication is that much needs to be done to help teachers become informed about what research is saying to them about their use of questions and questioning techniques in the classroom. Having and using this knowledge base is essential if decisions affecting appropriate instructional change linked to student achievement are to be considered. Gall (1984) strongly suggested that teacher educators need to be more actively and creatively involved in helping preservice and inservice teachers develop and improve interactive skills. An awareness and understanding of these skills, particularly the use of effective questions and questioning techniques, and how they influence students' achievement, is a major step toward that end.

REFERENCES

Berliner, D. "The Half-Full Glass: A Review of Research on Teaching." In *Using What We Know About Teaching*, edited by P. Hosford. Washington, D.C.: ASCD, 1984.

Bloom, B.S., et al., eds. *Taxonomy of Educational Objectives, Handbook I: Cognitive Domain*. New York: David McKay, 1956.

Brophy, J., and Good, T. "Teacher Behavior and Student Achievement." In *Handbook of Research on Teaching*, edited by M. Wittrock. 3d ed. New York: Macmillan, 1986.

Dillon, J. T. "Research on Questioning and Discussion." *Educational Leadership* 41 (November 1984): 50-56.

_____. *Teaching and the Art of Questioning*. Fastback Series 194. Bloomington, Ind.: Phi Delta Kappan, 1983.

Gall M. "Synthesis of Research on Teachers' Questioning." *Educational Leadership* 41 (November 1984): 40-47.

_____. "The Use of Questions in Teaching." *Review of Educational Research* 40 (1970): 707-21.

Hare, V.C., and Pulliam, C.A. "Teacher Questioning: A Verification and Extension." *Journal of Reading Behavior* 12 (1980): 69-72.

Hunkins, F.P. "Helping Students Ask Their Own Questions." *Social Education* 49 (April 1985): 293-96.

Levin, T., with Long, R. *Effective Instruction.* Washington, D.C.: ASCD, 1981.

Miller, B., and Johnson, J. *A Comparative View of the Role of Women.* Denver: Center for Teaching International Relations, University of Denver, 1976.

Mills, S.R.; Rice, C.; Berliner, D.; and Rousseau, E.W. "Correspondence Between Teacher Questions and Student Answers in Classroom Discourse." *Journal of Experimental Education* 48 (Spring 1980): 194-204.

Rowe, M.B. "Wait Time and Reward As Instructional Variables, Their Influence on Language, Logic and Fate Control: Part One—Wait Time." *Journal of Research on Science Teaching* 11 (1974): 81-94.

Swift, J.N., and Gooding, C.T. "Interaction of Wait Time Feedback and Questioning Instruction on Middle School Science Teaching." *Journal of Research in Science Teaching* 20 (1983): 721-30.

Weil, M., and Murphy, J. "Instructional Processes." *Encyclopedia of Educational Research*, 5th ed., 1982.

Wilen, W., and Clegg, A. "Effective Questions and Questioning: A Research Review." *Theory and Research in Social Education* 14 (Spring 1986): 153-61.

Wood, D., and Wood, H. "Questioning and Student Initiative." In *Questioning and Discussion: A Multidisciplinary Study*, edited by J. Dillon. Norwood, N.J.: Ablex Publishing, 1987.

7. DISCUSSION STRATEGIES AND TACTICS

by Ronald T. Hyman, Professor of Education, Rutgers University, New Brunswick, New Jersey

Consultant: Lawrence F. Lowery, Professor of Education, University of California, Berkeley

The characteristics, principles, types, and phases of discussion are examined. A discussion strategy is a plan involving a sequence of steps to achieve a goal, while tactics are questioning skills applied to facilitate the discussion. Questioning strategies for explaining, problem solving, debriefing, predicting, and policy-deciding discussions are presented and illustrated with classroom examples. A particular focus is placed on the fielding tactics teachers use to handle students' responses to questions.

Reality demands and theory prescribes that classroom teachers be competent in asking questions of their students because questioning is a basic skill in teaching. Reality also indicates that teachers ask questions in clusters, thereby forming the foundation for verbal interactions with students. Effective teachers cluster their questions and sequence them so as to maximize the pedagogical power of questioning. Pedagogical power emerges because the meaning and effect of any given question stems not from its individual structure or objective but from its context within the overall interaction between teacher and student. The outcome of using a carefully designed sequence of questions is cumulative strength, a synergistic effect. Based on such a conception of teacher questioning this chapter focuses on the strategies and tactics teachers utilize to enhance the quality of the verbal interaction they have with students.[1]

Teachers ask questions in the three major families of teaching methods—presenting (which includes lecturing as the prime constituent family member), enabling (which includes discussion), and exemplifying (which includes demonstrating), though they rely most on questions in the enabling family.[2] Indeed, it is impossible to conceive of leading a discussion without the asking of questions because questions are used to elicit and clarify alternative points of view, to involve the various participants, especially reticent or shy ones, to focus and direct the speakers' comments along desired lines, and to stimulate particular cognitive processes with the topic at hand. Though some people may advocate new technological innovations, the question remains the single best item in the teacher's collection of professional tools. Once the student is mentally prepared and perplexed, "the shock, the bite, of a question will force the mind to go wherever it is capable of going better than will the most ingenious pedagogical device unaccompanied by this mental ardor."[3] It is for this reason that questions are numerous in a discussion and also critical to shaping and effecting its success.[4]

ELEMENTS OF A DISCUSSION

A discussion is an interactive endeavor with a set of defining elements or characteristics that distinguishes it from other teaching methods. First and foremost, a discussion is a *social activity* involving more than one student *participating* in order to examine (1) the facts of a situation, (2) the consequences, meaning, and implications of the facts, and (3) alternative perspectives on the topic under study. Also, discussion is *cooperative* in that participants implicitly, if not explicitly, agree to explore the topic together in a thorough, *rational*, *purposeful* manner.[5] To do so the participants, under the leadership of the teacher, must be *systematic* and yet *creative* as they amend previous points and offer up new ones in light of previous comments and questions by participants and leader.

PHASES OF A DISCUSSION

No matter how brief it may be, a discussion ideally has three distinct phases, each with its own function and characteristics. It is necessary to recognize these three phases, to plan for them, and to execute them appropriately in order to achieve a sense of satisfaction and completion. The analogy with a well-designed meal comes to mind: appetizer or soup, main course, and dessert, every course providing a different type of food to satisfy the diner.

In a discussion, first comes the beginning phase with three subparts. To begin, the teacher (though technically it need not be the teacher) introduces the topic and proceeds to clarify it by setting limitations and specifying with some precision the nature of the topic. For example, suppose the topic is introduced broadly as "The United States and the UN." For the students to be able to follow the teacher and engage in the ensuing talk, they need to know which aspects of the relationship between the United States and the UN they are to pursue. Either the teacher must initiate the narrowing of the topic or a student must ask a question for clarification. In either case, the result eventually *should be in question form* and might be something like: "Today we will be talking about the position of the United States as a leading world power and the probable consequences of the United States withdrawing from the UN. If you wish, we can even discuss whether the United States should withdraw at this point from the UN, given the condition of world politics and the workings of the UN as an institution. So today we'll be discussing the question, What will happen if the United States withdraws from the UN?"

In the second subpart, the participants decide on procedure. Most often, in classrooms teachers alone make this decision and do so implicitly by the very way they lead. However, it need not be so. Indeed, the teacher can, and is wise to, quickly request students to help structure the discussion. Such a step is an effective way to involve the students and to create the valid feeling that they have a stake in what will transpire.

In the third subpart, which completes the initial phase, some participant must make an assertion on the narrowed topic for it is this assertion that ignites interaction among discussants. For example, whether by self-initiation or in response to a question, a student might say, "If the United States were to withdraw from the UN now, the UN would collapse because it is already weak due to its poor finances ever since the United States began paying only one-half its annual dues assessment."

In the middle phase of a discussion, the participants pursue the initial assertions that have been made by examining them, modifying them, and offering additional ones. The specific subparts of the middle phase of a given discussion depend upon the type of discussion that is occurring. We shall pursue five main types of discussion shortly.

In order to be effective, the end phase of a discussion does not merely stop but it ends appropriately, signaling to the participants that the end has arrived. Just as the dessert signals the end of the meal and a coda the end of a sonata, the three subparts of the end phase of the discussion close the discussion in a satisfying manner. The participants draw conclusions, someone recapitulates the main points made, and someone (generally the teacher) launches new activities that arise from or are related to the discussion that took place.

In summary, then, there is a general structure to all discussions:

1. Beginning Phase
   a. Introducing and clarifying the question for discussion
   b. Setting procedure
   c. Making initial assertions on the topic

2. Middle Phase
   Examining the assertions made (subparts of this phase differ depending on the type of discussion)

3. End Phase
   a. Drawing conclusions
   b. Recapitulating
   c. Launching new activities

TYPES OF DISCUSSION

As indicated, there are different types of discussion even though it is possible to identify a general structure to be used in all discussions. The five most common and useful types to note are explaining, problem solving, debriefing, predicting, and policy deciding. The labels indicate the purposes of these types and suggest the different paths participants will take as they respond to the guiding questions of the teacher, beginning with the carefully phrased topic question.

1. *Explaining:* analyzes the causes, reasons, procedures, or methods for what has occurred. For example, (1) "Why have terrorist activities increased in the past 20 years?" (2) "How did Japan become an electronic giant since 1945?"

138

2. *Problem solving:* seeks to answer a conflict or problem facing the group or the larger community outside the classroom. For example, (1) "How can we decrease sexism—male and female sexism—in our school?" (2) "How can the federal government win its battle against illegal drugs?"

3. *Debriefing:* reflects on the facts, meaning, and implications of a shared activity such as a trip to the Statue of Liberty, a view of the play or film *Death of a Salesman*, participation in a mock 4–H convention, or hearing a guest speaker from NASA on "Space Travel in the Next Century." For example, "Let's now discuss our trip to the Statue of Liberty. What did we see and then what does it all mean?"

4. *Predicting:* predicts the probable consequences of a given situation, condition, or policy. For example, (1) "If the greenhouse effect on our planet continues, what will happen to the plant and animal life, as we know it today?" (2) "What are the implications for humankind now that twentieth-century medicine has increased the average length of life to about 65 years?"

5. *Policy deciding:* sets policy on how the group should act or recommends policy for the larger community outside the classroom. For example, (1) "Should we *as a class* participate in our town's protest parade next Tuesday against the state government building a dam here on Silver Creek?" (2) "Should the United States government ban cigarette smoking in the entire country?"

For teachers to succeed in leading any one of the five types of discussion, it is necessary for them to go beyond knowledge about elements, phases, and types of discussion. It is essential that teachers become strategic in applying their knowledge. To do so they must have familiarity and skill with some basic strategies which they can subsequently refine to suit their own personal needs and the particular characteristics of their students. Thus, it is to the topic of strategy and tactics, especially strategic questionings, that we now turn.

STRATEGY AND TACTICS

A strategy is a carefully prepared plan involving a sequence of steps designed to achieve a given goal. A strategy is important because it provides a framework within which to determine which materials to use and which questions to ask before the discussion begins and especially as the discussion proceeds. The interaction between teacher and student is so complex and generally so rapid as to prevent long deliberations. The ability at a given juncture in the discussion to ask an appropriate question, one that will continue the forward thrust of the interaction, requires a framework. A strategy reduces the strain on the teacher in the midst of the discussion and moreover provides a cumulative effect for spurring students on to think fruitfully.

A strategy for a discussion on, for example, the desirability of United States withdrawal from the UN will include more than the strategic, key questions that the teacher will ask to guide the students. The questioning strategy is fundamental and the heart of the overall strategy, but it is simply not enough. Teachers must also include steps to be taken regarding the roles of the various participants, their own roles, the procedure to be used for eliciting initial assertions to serve as the discussion's springboard, allocation of time to crucial points, means of involving participants in open exchanges, arrangement of people and furniture in the available space, and utilization of human and audio-visual resources.

For example, in regard to roles, the teacher must plan strategically for a way to get initial assertions on the floor. Suppose that the class will see the play *Death of a Salesman*, and the teacher will lead a debriefing discussion upon return to the classroom. The teacher may wish to use one of the following tactics (*a tactic is a small-scale element of the strategy*): (1) before or during the trip the teacher will arrange with one or a pair of students to be designated first speakers; or (2) on return to the classroom the teacher will request all students to write one sentence describing the character who impressed them the most (or whom they understood the best or with whom they identified strongly); or (3) the teacher will request each student to complete the following sentence stem to be shared with the class, "From seeing *Death of a Salesman*, I realize that Willy Loman _____." In short, the teacher must plan to have a student or students make the initial assertions of the discussion. The teacher must also consider such roles as designated first speaker, summarizer, presenter of a prepared statement, timekeeper, and reactor to comments and conclusions drawn.

The questioning strategy for a discussion serves as the heart of the discussion, the middle phase, as it pumps critical questions before the participants for them to respond to. Several questioning strategies are illustrated in Figures 7-1 through 7-5. Some overall points about these strategies are in order before dealing with each one specifically.

140

1. Each strategy is a general strategy that requires modification to suit the particular students, teacher, and course.
2. On the left side are listed the questions to be asked, primarily by the teacher, but they may be raised by students themselves, thus obviating the need for the teacher to ask them. On the right side are listed the cognitive processes that the students perform as they respond to the questions. This arrangement provides an easy visual guide to what the strategy seeks to achieve.
3. The questions listed are only the foundational, core questions. The teacher will no doubt ask several minor followup questions as the discussion moves along, in order to clarify and probe specific points raised in the students' responses to the key questions.
4. Each strategy includes a variety of question types, thereby leading the students to perform a variety of cognitive tasks.[6]

The five questioning strategies correspond to the five types of discussion identified earlier. This does not in any way mean that only these five questioning strategies fit the five discussion types. Nor does it mean that these are the only five questioning strategies possible. Rather, it does mean that these five serve only as examples of strategies that teachers can and should design to help them lead discussions. To be sure, there are other strategies for such purposes as explaining how to do something, explaining the cause of an event, resolving value conflicts, and developing concepts inductively.[7]

Figure 7-1 presents a questioning strategy for analyzing a work of fiction and is to be used in an *explaining* discussion. This analysis strategy begins with the basic step of identifying and describing the central features of the work in order to create a common ground for all participants to build upon. It leads the students to relate, analyze, compare, and synthesize points. It requires students to make both intrawork and interwork comparisons as they consider previous responses. By following this strategy, the teacher is not restricted to a mere recounting of the story but has a plan for analysis and connection of the work of fiction with previous material studied, the students' preferences in fiction, and the students' own lives.

Figure 7-2 presents a questioning strategy for a *problem-solving* discussion. As does the strategy on policy deciding, this strategy begins with the necessary step of careful delineation of the problem itself. The significance of this strategy lies in the request by the questioner to offer alternate solutions to the identified problem. In this way, students learn

Figure 7-1. Questioning Strategy for Analyzing a Work of Fiction

Questioner	Respondent
1. Who are the main characters and what are the main events of this story (book)?	1. Identifies and describes the central features.
2. What are the connections between the main characters, events, location, and time of this story?	2. Relates the central features to each other.
3. In what ways did the main characters change during the story?	3. Identifes movement in the story.
4. How did these changes affect the other characters and the events in the story?	4. Analyzes the effects of change on other elements in the story.
5. Were you expecting the story to end as it did? If yes, how did the author prepare you for the ending? If no, how did the author surprise you?	5. Compares the expected ending to the author's ending.
6. How did the author create and maintain your interest in the story?	6. Analyzes the elements of style that characterize the author in this story.
7. How are the elements (events, people, and setting) of this story similar to elements in your own life? How are they different?	7. Compares and relates the story to his or her own life.
8. In what ways is this story like "(title)" or some other story you have read?	8. Compares this story to another story.
9. What is your favorite short passage from the book? Tell what qualities it has.	9. Identifies and comments on a passage that is liked.
10. What do you conclude about this story in light of the points you've made already?	10. Synthesizes the many points raised and draws a conclusion.

SOURCE: "Questioning for Improved Reading," by R. T. Hyman, *Educational Leadership* 39 (January 1982): 39. Reprinted with permission.

Figure 7-2. Questioning Strategy for Problem Solving

Questioner	Respondent
1. What precisely is the problem confronting us?	1. Describes the problem.
2. What, in your opinion, are the chief causes of the problem?	2. Identifies events and conditions leading to the problem.
3. What are the relevant facts of the problem that are connected with the causes identified?	3. Relates the problem to the causes, thereby interpreting the problem under consideration.
4. What action do you recommend to solve this problem?	4. Suggests a solution.
5. What support do you have that your recommended action will solve the problem?	5. Justifies the recommendation.
6. If we took that action, what else might occur?	6. Predicts other probable consequences.
7. Based on the various points raised, what do you conclude is the best or appropriate way to solve the problem?	7. Draws conclusion among alternative solutions proposed.

SOURCE: Adapted by permission of the publisher from R. T. Hyman, *Improving Discussion Leadership* (New York: Teachers College Press, copyright 1980 by Teachers College, Columbia University; all rights reserved), p. 45.

Figure 7-3. Questioning Strategy for Debriefing an Activity

Questioner	Respondent
1. What are some of the specifics that occurred to you during the activity (field trip, film, play, debate, simulation) such as events you observed, decisions you made, and feelings you had?	1. Describes some details of the activity, making them public knowledge.
2. What did you learn about the situation, yourself, and other people from this activity?	2. States the personal interpretation of the activity.
3. What are the key ideas that this activity teaches us?	3. States the concepts or generalizations that give meaning or purpose to the activity.
4. In what ways are the actions, rules, events, facts, and outcomes of this activity similar to those in other parts of your life?	4. Compares and contrasts the activity with other events of the world.
5. In what ways could we change this activity to improve it or make it more like the real events? (This question applies to some activities such as a film, play, simulation, and the like but may not apply to other types of activity being debriefed.)	5. Suggests modifications that will improve the activity or make it closer to the real world.
6. What do you conclude from all these actions and points made?	6. Summarizes and concludes about the entire activity.

SOURCE: *Strategic Questioning*, by R. T. Hyman (with modifications) (Englewood Cliffs, N.J.: Prentice-Hall, 1975); pp. 93-94. Copyright © 1975 by R. T. Hyman.

Figure 7-4. Questioning Strategy for Predicting

Questioner	Respondent
1. What precisely is the situation we're concerned with—its features and conditions?	1. Describes the situation.
2. Given that this situation exists or will exist, what do you think will happen as a result? (What are the probable consequences of this situation?)	2. Predicts a new situation or event.
3. What facts and generalizations support your prediction?	3. Supports the prediction by applying a generalization and related facts.
4. What other things might happen as a result of this situation?	4. Offers an alternative prediction.
5. If the predicted situation occurs, what will happen next?	5. Gives some consequences of the prediction.
6. In summary, what will lead us from the current situation to your predicted one?	6. Summarizes by showing the connections fundamental to the prediction.

SOURCE: *Strategic Questioning*, by R. T. Hyman (Englewood Cliffs, N.J.: Prentice-Hall, 1975); p. 71. Copyright © 1975 by R. T. Hyman.

Figure 7-5. Questioning Strategy to Decide on Policy

Questioner	Respondent
1. What precisely is the issue before us?	1. Identifies and describes the issue.
2. What is your stand on the issue at this point?	2. Expresses an opinion, position.
3. What are the key words used in talking about this issue?	3. Identifies the central concepts.
4. Define the key terms.	4. Defines the essential terms for clarity of communication.
5. What are your goals about this situation, your desired state of affairs?	5. Establishes an ideal.
6. What are the relevant facts, current and past, on this issue?	6. States pertinent evidence for support of the position.
7. How would you implement the stand (action, policy) you take?	7. Examines the issue from a practical, interactive viewpoint.
8. What are the probable consequences of your stand? (What is likely to happen as a result of your action?)	8. Predicts some consequences of the position taken.
9. What would be your position if you were person X (name a specific person or group of persons)?	9. Sees the issue from another perspective.
10. What are some other possible positions to take?	10. Describes some alternatives.
11. What are the probable consequences of each of these alternatives?	11. Predicts some consequences of the various alternatives.

SOURCE: *Strategic Questioning*, by R. T. Hyman (Englewood Cliffs, N.J.: Prentice-Hall, 1975); pp. 90-91. Copyright © 1975 by R. T. Hyman.

Figure 7-5. Questioning Strategy to Decide on Policy (Continued)

Questioner	Respondent
12. In what ways is your stand on this issue related to another issue or position you've taken previously?	12. Sees connections with a parallel situation for a possible genral principle.
13. In light of all these points, what stand do you take on this issue now?	13. Expresses an opinion based on the previous points.
14. What are the key points that lead you to this position?	14. Gives reasons; justifies the position taken.

that problems such as nuclear power plant accidents, illegal drugs, and raising money to fight birth defects—and even problems of a lesser scale—are complex and do not have simple, pure solutions. In the end, students learn that whoever presents a solution must choose that solution from a group of alternative solutions based on the desirability of the probable consequences of the various proposed solutions.

Figure 7-3 presents a questioning strategy for *debriefing* an activity. Although similar to the others, it has one unique aspect regarding activities such as a film, play, or simulation. This strategy even applies to an activity such as a debate or game where the participants can identify an ideal example of the activity. That is to say, this strategy leads the respondents to compare the activity with the real world (in the case of an activity that is designed to simulate or represent the real world) or to compare it with the ideal (in the case of an activity where an ideal or better example can be specified). In this way, the respondents are led to examine the model inherent in their activity and to relate it to the real world or to the ideal. Through reflection, comparison, and suggested modifications, the students learn from the raw activity as they build upon it.

Figure 7-4 presents a strategy for *predicting* what will happen as a result of a given event or situation, either now or in the immediate future. In other words, "Given A, predict B." The strategy begins with as precise a description of the situation as possible. This allows the students to perceive how they variously understand the situation and eventually to understand how their various perspectives influence the predictions made. The strategy also requires that students identify the facts and generalizations that they have used in support of their predictions. This is a key step in order to teach implicitly that predictng is not merely guessing but a rational consideration of the situation, its features, related facts, and the probable consequences of today's conditions. In this way, students apply previously made generalizations and also learn to think about alternative outcomes and predictions, since it is impossible to predict with 100 percent accuracy because of the complexity of the world.

Figure 7-5 offers a strategy for leading students to *decide on policy* regarding a particular issue, such as the development and use of nuclear energy or the legalization of smoking marijuana. Because deciding on policy in a reasoned way requires consideration of a complex set of variables, this strategy is long in terms of the number of steps and the time needed to complete it. The strategy is also complex in that it requires the students to offer definitions, facts, explanations, comparisons, opinions, and justifications.

It is also significant that this strategy twice—Steps 2 and 13—asks the students to take a stand. The initial request in Step 2 comes in order to demonstrate the range of positions possible, to acknowledge the fact that people do have opinions on issues whether or not they arrive at them after careful consideration of the pertinent information, and most of all to involve the students in the issue by requiring a commitment or stake at the outset even though it may only be temporary. The second request comes in Step 13 in order to demonstrate that people have the right to modify their decisions in light of the many points raised in the discussion. Indeed, the strategy implicitly teaches that it is reasonable to be influenced by others during a deliberation.

Fielding

To implement a discussion strategy, especially the questioning strategy as the central middle phase, teachers need smaller-scale steps called tactics. Chapters 4, 5, 6, and 8, which the reader is urged to read, treat in some detail questioning skills, which are virtually synonymous with questioning tactics. Therefore, this section will treat only those tactics that are reactive and flow from an initial asking of a question. To do so it is necessary to introduce the concept of *fielding*, that is, the ways in which a speaker handles or deals with a response to the question asked.[8] Thus, we shall deal with how the teacher can and should field the responses offered by the students to the key questions of the questioning strategy being used.

There is a sizable and still growing literature on teacher questioning and rightly so. There is currently only a small amount written about teacher fielding. Yet, the way a teacher fields a student response may turn out to influence the discussion more strongly than the teacher's initiating question. For instance, suppose that the teacher asks during a debriefing discussion of a trip to the Statue of Liberty (see Figure 7-3), "What are the key ideas that this trip teaches us?" Suppose further that the student responds, "When I first saw her up close from the boat, I was amazed at how tall she is—like she was standing there over me, to guard me." The teacher should field this response, not with anger or annoyance or verbal chastisement of the student for not answering the question, but rather, in a way that recognizes that the respondent was not quite ready cognitively to move to generalizing abstractions about the Statue of Liberty. The student was still "ventilating" about the trip and was responding to question one of that strategy.

With a fielding tactic that leads that respondent and the others to move cooperatively and respectfully from their concrete experiences to some generalizations, the teacher can continue to foster active participation and the ultimate achievement of the goal of the discussion. With a fielding move that conveys annoyance or sarcasm, for example, the teacher might well exclude that particular respondent and others who are also not ready to move to question three of the debriefing. In fact, the teacher might well strangle the entire discussion with such a negative fielding move that the students cease to participate in reaction to the teacher's inappropriate tactic.

Just as there are options for the teacher in deciding which type of discussion to lead and which type of question to ask a given student, so are there options in fielding. There are no firm prescriptive rules for deciding how to field or when to use a particular fielding tactic. Nevertheless, there is a guideline for teachers to follow: field so as to promote the elements and principles of discussion positively. That is, the teacher should foster and strengthen the elements, for example, of cooperation and participation. The teacher must make quick, on-the-spot decisions depending on the context of the discussion, the particular students, and the teacher's purpose for the discussion. Teachers can make these decisions appropriately once they have a sensitivity to the importance of fielding, the guideline for fielding student responses, and a repertoire of tactical fielding options.

Below is a list of seven fielding tactics that teachers can employ during discussions. There are others, but at this point these appear to constitute a basic set that teachers should feel comfortable with and can use. Teachers may field student responses to key questions by:

1. Probing the respondent for clarification or elaboration.[9]
2. Probing for clarification or elaboration by calling on students other than the respondent to the question.
3. Asking the same question again so as to elicit multiple responses to the key question.[10]
4. Waiting silently for 3 to 5 seconds to encourage other students to comment on the response, add to it, or contribute their responses on their own initiative.[11]
5. Designating a student to comment on, agree with, or disagree with the respondent in light of previous remarks of both students.

6. Themselves clarifying, elaborating, agreeing with, or disagreeing with the response.
7. Evaluating the response (hopefully in positive terms) with strong and pertinent comments.[12]

With these fielding tactics combined with the questioning skills presented in the other chapters, the knowledge about discussion in terms of elements, phases, and types, and the questioning strategies offered earlier in this chapter, teachers have some basic tools to use in leading discussions with their students. As with such tools as a hammer, saw, and wrench, it is the task of the teacher to master the use of the tools so as to become a professional who performs excellently in discussions. As the ancient Indian saying goes, "Everyone uses tools, but the artist does so with skill and taste."

NOTES

[1]This chapter is drawn primarily from my two books on the topic: *Strategic Questioning* (Englewood Cliffs, N.J.: Prentice-Hall, 1979) and *Improving Discussion Leadership* (New York: Teachers College Press, 1980).

[2]See Chapter 7 of my *Strategic Questioning* for a detailed treatment of these three families of teaching methods.

[3]John Dewey, *How We Think* (Lexington, Mass.: D.C. Heath, 1933), pp. 268-69.

[4]C. J. B. Macmillan and J. W. Garrison go so far as to propose a concept of teaching based on student question asking and teacher answering. See their article "An Erotetic Concept of Teaching," *Educational Theory* 33 (Summer/Fall 1983): 157-66, and the responses to it in the same journal, 36 (Fall 1986): 343-61.

[5]For the effects and value of a cooperative environment, see the recent works by Alfie Kohn which present a review of recent studies by the leading researchers on the topic: "How To Succeed Without Even Vying," *Psychology Today* 20, no. 9 (September 1986): 22-28, and *No Contest: The Case Against Competition* (Boston: Houghton Mifflin, 1986). See also the 1984 publication, *Perspectives on Effective Teaching and the Cooperative Classroom*, edited by Judy Reinhartz (Washington, D.C.: National Education Association, 1984).

[6]A detailed treatment of questions that elicit various cognitive types is presented in Chapter 4 by Roger T. Cunningham.

[7] See my *Strategic Questioning* and two books by Jack P. Fraenkel for more questioning strategies: *Helping Students Think and Value* (Englewood Cliffs, N.J.: Prentice-Hall, 1973), and *How To Teach About Values* (Englewood Cliffs, N.J.: Prentice-Hall, 1977).

[8] For an explanation of the concept of fielding and its application to student questions, see Ronald T. Hyman, "Fielding Student Questions," *Theory into Practice* 19, no. 1 (Winter 1980): 38-44.

[9] For various types of probing questions, especially alternatives to the use of why as a probe, see pp. 113-30 of my *Strategic Questioning*.

[10] See the research which shows the positive effect of eliciting multiple student responses in Frank L. Ryan, "The Effects on Social Studies Achievement of Multiple Student Responding to Different Levels of Questioning," *Journal of Experimental Education* 4, no. 4 (Summer 1974): 71-75.

[11] See the section on wait time in Chapter 5 by Mary Budd Rowe.

[12] For research data on classroom tone (affect) related to the need for strong and pertinent comments, see John I. Goodlad, "A Study of Schooling: Some Findings and Hypotheses," *Phi Delta Kappan* 64, no. 7 (March 1983): 467, and Kenneth A. Sirotnik, "What You See Is What You Get: Consistency, Persistency, and Mediocrity in Classrooms," *Harvard Educational Review* 53, no. 1 (February 1983): 21.

8. STUDENTS AS KEY QUESTIONERS

by Francis P. Hunkins, Professor of Education, University of Washington, Seattle

Consultant: Katherine Cornbleth, Department of Learning and Instruction, College of Education, State University of New York at Buffalo

Students are natural questioners because of their inquisitiveness. Approaches teachers can take to create an educational environment that encourages and facilitates students' questioning are examined. A questioning cycle of planning, implementing, and assessing is presented to help organize students to work with questions. Three questioning strategies that can be taught directly to students within the classroom setting are presented for teachers to assist students to structure their questions and thinking.

Once you have learned how to ask questions, relevant and appropriate and substantial questions, you have learned how to learn and no one can keep you from learning whatever you want or need to know. (Postman and Weingartner 1963)

Currently there is much discussion about providing educational experiences that will allow students to become active learners who are in control of their approaches to learning, who can learn what they want to learn. The thrust is to enable students to delve into data, to seek the relevance of their investigations and the payoff of learning. Present educational dialog centers on ways to give students those skills and competencies requisite for active learning, not only in school situations but in their outside worlds.

Central to enabling students to be active, successful learners is to make sure that they are aware of and skilled in formulating questions and questioning strategies. This requires that students comprehend the concept of questions and the fundamental means-ends relationship extant between responding to questions and one's understanding of the material questioned. It is true that children come to school as question askers. However, they are unaware of the various types of questions and the cognitive processes activated when answering questions. Children do not have a real command of the procedural knowledge requisite for processing data so as to further their understanding of material encountered (Gavelek and Raphael 1969).

QUESTIONS

The question is a specialized type of sentence that serves an interrogative function. It provides the questioner with an instructional cue conveying to him or her what is to be learned and possible ways of approaching particular material. The question enables the questioner to make clear his or her orientation to particular information. A well-stated question suggests to its asker a potential answer. But a question also suggests certain assumptions. Dillon (1986) notes that questions and questioning deal with two kinds of assumptions: presuppositions and presumptions.

He indicates that presuppositions are a logical property of the question itself. All questions communicate to the person being questioned what the asker assumes. The person raising a question assumes that there is an answer and that the answer lies within a particular sphere. It is for this reason that a question can be processed.

A second type of prior assumption that Dillon asserts all questions contain is a presumption. A person raising a question in the classroom informs those to whom the question is addressed that certain situations exist. One situation is that there is an answer and that is is possible for the person being questioned to respond correctly. Also presumed is that there is sufficient time and adequate and appropriate material to process the question in the most meaningful manner. Further, the question being posed presumes that the person either asking the question or being asked the question has a desire to know its answer.

Questions can faciliate an individual's thinking, enabling active participation in learning. The particular level of intellectual functioning is influenced in part by the cognitive level of the question. Most commonly, questions are classified according to the cognitive function they are intended to elicit in the person either using or responding to the question. Bloom's (1956) categories of knowledge, comprehension, application, analysis, synthesis, and evaluation are well known. Hyman (1979) classified questions as definitional, empirical, evaluative, and metaphysical. Definitional questions are really knowledge questions. Such questions request persons to define a word, term, or phrase. Empirical questions require the respondee to react in terms of perceptions of the world. The questions invite the respondee to furnish facts, compare and contrast, and interpret and explain events and inferences. Evaluative questions ask one to praise, blame, commend, criticize, or rate something, drawing on personal value judgments. Metaphysical questions solicit responses drawing on metaphysical or theological beliefs. Such questions involve faith. Chapter 4 of this book provides another classification system based on levels of convergent and divergent questions.

These three classifications of questions place questions within a cognitive hierarchy from knowledge of facts to judgments about conclusions. Christenbury and Kelly (1983), classifying questions by focus, present a contrasting organizer. They put questions into overlapping areas of matter, personal reality, and external reality. Questions within the matter realm focus on the subject of discussion. Personal reality questions require responses based on personal experiences, values, and ideas. Questions contained within external reality call for reflection on the external world: other peoples' experiences and histories.

While most question classifications are cognitive, questions can be classified in affective terms as well. Krathwohl's (1964) taxonomy is well known to most: attending, responding, valuing, organization, and characterization. Such questions request from individuals how they perceive their reality, their value base, their outlook on life. Another system to classify affective questions is provided in Chapter 4 of this book.

Questions are powerful vehicles for processing information. Students with mastery of these linguistic vehicles are in command of their learning. Persons with such control are thinkers and questioners; they possess a healthy skepticism. They are not overly dependent upon teachers and other authorities for the focus of learning, for their questions. Persons aware of the power of questions and the nature of questions will be able to prepare educative questions, questions that have the power to initiate and guide learning (Dillon 1983). Students skilled in questions will have the confidence to investigate data knowing full well that questions appropriate to a search will furnish answers that will reveal the unknown. Students in control of their questions will be clear as to why they are phrasing them.

Gavelek and Raphael (1985) identified five skills that, when mastered, make one a competent performer with information—a good questioner. The first skill refers to students being adept at determining their understanding of questions raised by others. In order to make this assessment, students require a sophistication about questions and question-answering strategies. This skill can be directly taught to students.

Another skill exhibited by competent performers, questioners, is possessing awareness of the various information sources available that are relevant to the questions being raised. Related to this skill is assessing or evaluating the appropriateness of information encountered in relation to questions asked. Successful students realize that their background information is a most useful source of information.

The third major skill of competent students relates to assessing the adequacy of their own levels of knowledge. Here students are capable of inquiring as to what they know or do not know. In this situation, students can map out those areas that require their attention.

Another skill of effective students is the ability to process the questions of others, either the teacher's or those of authors of textbooks or other written material. Such students employ questions to determine what is important and thus worthy of attention.

The final question-anwering skill deals with the "criterion problem." This refers to a student's recognition of the completeness of an answer to a particular question in contrast to its being accurate but not complete. Students who have not mastered this skill may stop their search upon finding the first accurate "bit" of information to a question, thus neglecting further answers necessary for obtaining the "whole story."

STUDENTS' QUESTIONS

Educators testify to the importance of students being effective questioners; however, teachers' behavior often belies this position. Much research on questioning has shown that the teacher, not the student, is the key questioner in the classroom. When students are encouraged to ask questions, their questions reflect an overemphasis on specific knowledge of facts. Students have been conditioned to be content solely with finding out how many and when and who, rather than with identifying unstated assumptions, flaws in an argument, or meaningful relationships among data. Students have been conditioned to pursue knowing information rather than thinking about and truly understanding information.

Students can be skillful questioners if we will but allow them opportunities for questioning. But, for opportunity to be scheduled we must trust students, trust them to be inquisitive, to desire to learn in particular ways to maintain or enhance the self, to make use of the resources that will advance particular inquiries (Rogers 1951). To be skillful questioners, students require opportunities to generate questions, to be engaged in what Singer (1978) has identified as "active comprehension." They need time to reflect on questions generated to identify the presumptions brought to questioning. Students need time to consider appropriate strategies and they need to realize that when posing a question, they are making a statement of who they are and what they know in relation to the world.

SETTING THE STAGE FOR STUDENTS' QUESTIONS

Students are natural questioners, commencing their educational experiences with high inquisitiveness. To build on this natural tendency to question requires an educational environment that facilitates students' questioning. Basic to creating and maintaining such an atmosphere is that both teacher and students express confidence in each other as people and as questioners.

Getting Students to Be Key Questioners

A good atmosphere for student questioning exhibits personal respect for the ideas and concerns of all. There is an openness to new views. Students realize that they are free to raise questions at any level and that they, as class members, must allow others to generate questions. Everyone's question is legitimate, if phrased for a purpose. If students' questions are interpreted as signs of failure or of inattention, there will be few student questions. The productive atmosphere encourages the exchange of ideas and questions in nonthreatening ways. Both teacher and students listen to each other—to each other's questions. All parties are willing to assist and to be enthusiastic about helping classmates with their questions and questioning. There is an *esprit de corps* among the questioners.

In a good atmosphere, all parties realize that questions and questioning are integral parts of the learning process. The teacher, in creating a good questioning atmosphere, has informed and allowed students to discover the nature of ignorance and the value of recognizing it. Accepting ignorance fosters a true spirit of inquiry. It further allows students to appreciate the complexity of knowledge. Ignorance, a natural state, is being uninformed, lacking knowledge. Recognizing and accepting being uninformed is the first condition for engaging in inquiry, in raising questions. It allows one to set a baseline for dealing with awe and wonder. It defines an arena for open exploration.

Accepting ignorance as a necessary first step is done with the realization that it is not total ignorance. Miyake and Norman (1979) pointed this out in their article, "To Ask a Question, One Must Know Enough to Know What Is Not Known." In raising their own questions, students must identify those aspects of the information confronted that are not well understood by them or that require attention at this particular "learning moment."

Miyake and Norman point out that there is an apparent dilemma in that students must understand enough to realize that which is not known. The skillful teacher employs several instructional approaches to assist students in dealing with this dilemma. Students can be told that in dealing with entirely new areas of information, the questions of others can be employed to direct their attention to important information. These questions raised by outsiders also can provide "hints" as to how the questions should be processed. All students can react to others' questions based on whether they know anything about the area questioned. Dealing with these questions, students increase their information base about the material being processed and then can raise questions to assess just how their level of understanding is changing.

Another way that students can deal with this apparent dilemma is to draw on incidental information they bring to school. All students, just from living in the world, have varying degrees of information about myriad issues and topics. Teachers can encourage students to "take stock" of this information. Teachers can make links between the new information of the lesson and some content or situations with which students are already familiar. Students may not know anything about a botany topic slated for study, but most will have walked in a field and have seen plants growing. Drawing on such experiences, students can raise questions even though they possess limited knowlege about the botany topic (Miyake and Norman 1979).

Teachers can also take advantage of what some have called "incidental comprehension"—comprehension that results without much thought just from reacting to others' questions, either heard or read. The skillful teacher informs students that they have more knowledge about some topics than they at first realize (Gavelek and Raphael 1985).

Essentially, the successful questioning environment furnishes students with tips regarding information to be investigated. Teachers make provocative statements designed to pique students' interests. Around the classroom, interest centers entice students to investigate further. Preliminary reading, using other's questions, can be assigned solely for generating questions rather than answers.

A positive questioning atmosphere also reflects a certain leisure. There is no rush to complete assignments, to process questions as rapidly as possible. There exists no academic race. There is time to consider the total situation. Students have time to reflect on the focus topic, time to formulate questions meaningful to the search. Students have opportunities to be playful with information, time to gather sufficient background data. A leisurely atmosphere is unpressured, affording students opportunities to generate questions that might be pursued. There is time to synthesize the results of questioning and to take a stand. A leisurely atmosphere says to students "savor your question formulation, relish your search, take satisfaction in the results of your investigation. Feel good about being the effective student, the effective questioner."

A classroom atmosphere conducive to good questions and questioning is one in which students realize that they share responsibility for their learning. There is independence of functioning. Students do not always wait for the teacher to act. They know that oftentimes it is their responsibility, their privilege, even their enjoyment to map out their involvement with information.

A playful questioning atmosphere can arise when students play questioning games. Students can challenge their classmates to solve a problem of the day. "Questions of interest to me" can be scheduled. Answers or statements can be written on the board with the teacher challenging students to discover the question. Teachers and students can place pictures around the classroom with the request "What is my question?"

Even the room arrangement can add positively to a questioning atmosphere. Students arranged in rows with the teacher at the front of the room are usually not encouraged to discuss or question with anyone but the teacher. Students seated in circles or semicircles have eye contact with their class colleagues and thus can interact more easily. Students can continue a dialog or a questioning sequence with such seating in place. Effective questioning and communication depends in part on students reading head nods, smiles, and frowns.

More than a decade ago this writer suggested a list of questions to consider to determine whether we are creating in our classrooms good places for questions. The list still is appropriate:

Did I provide an atmosphere that was nonthreatening and encouraged students to "blue sky" about the questions they wished to ask?

Did I schedule opportunities for students to discuss their questions with fellow classmates, with me?

Did I encourage student discussion of the consequences of the questions they asked?

Did I offer specific suggestions to students about how to plan, recognize, and implement particular question types into certain strategies for processing information?

Did I provide students with opportunities to test their questions in role playing or simulation?

Did I, as the teacher, serve as an effective exemplar of the good questioner?

Did I sit down with particular students or the class and discuss the dimensions of particular strategies and the place of the question in these strategies?

Did I discuss with students the task of analyzing questions they encountered in written materials?

Did I schedule opportunities for students to react cognitively and affectively to questions encountered or planned?

Did I give guidance to students in judging their questions on cognitive and affective levels?

Did I provide adequate time for questioning to take place? (Hunkins 1976).

160

QUESTIONING CYCLE

Students need an organizer for working with questions. A useful paradigm students can employ consists of three stages: planning, implementing, and assessing (Hunkins 1976). The planning stage involves activities that assist students in preparing for some learning encounter or investigation. It is during this stage that students identify the key questions they wish to investigate and map out the procedure or procedures to deal with the questions. This assumes that the students have received direct instruction in questions and the "how" of dealing with questions. The implementation stage involves the actual application of questions and procedures identified during planning. It is the *doing* phase of working with questions. It is the enactment of questions and questioning procedures. This stage makes students aware of their procedures and of the need to monitor their approaches to information. At the final stage, assessing, students critically think about the results of their investigation, evaluate the data gathered and the conclusions reached, and also attend to the appropriateness of questions employed and strategies used. This is the stage where students demonstrate their skill in dealing with the criterion problem.

SPECIFIC QUESTIONING STRATEGIES

Hyman (1979) identifies a strategy as "...a carefully prepared plan involving a sequence of steps designed to achieve a given goal." It furnishes the user with a guide for determining not only what questions to raise in the classroom but their particular sequence. It provides the framework around which the classroom interaction will take place. It allows for structured dialog with questions so placed as to give it cohesion and purpose. While Hyman addressed the teacher, such information is also useful to students. Students can employ strategies to structure their questions and their reflection. Following are three question strategies that can be directly taught to students.

Bloom's Taxonomic Strategy

Bloom's *Taxonomy of Educational Objectives* (1956), that is most familiar, allows us to classify our questions and place them in a questioning strategy. Proceeding through the steps from knowledge to evaluation, we have an inductive strategy. Reversing the steps from evaluation to synthesis down to knowledge gives us a deductive strategy. To get students to use the strategy, we first need to point out or have them discover the strategy. Here is a procedural structure that will allow them to process information at the level of the particular and proceed to the level of the general or the reverse. Students learn that questions can be formulated at various cognitive levels. Students require time to perfect formulating various types of questions. Students must know the difference between a comprehension question and an analysis or synthesis question to be successful in employing either the inductive or deductive strategy.

For students to utilize this strategy, they require planning time to determine their questions and whether to map them out in an inductive or deductive mode. Often students are not allowed time to reflect on what they wish to investigate, what questions they want to address, or to map out on paper any actual question sequence. Once students have mapped out their questions in a type of flow chart, then they can implement their plan—that is, carry out the strategy sketched on paper. Again, time must be allowed; the atmosphere should not be hurried. Students should have the opportunity to proceed down various investigatory avenues, to back up, to start again, and then to take some risks in formulating conclusions. Finally, students need time to assess the effectiveness of the strategy and their employment of it.

Assume that students in junior high school are dealing with a geography lesson on Australia focusing on the use of agricultural resources within the country. One or more students might note the following possible knowledge questions: "What is Australia's land area? What are the major land forms of the region? What are the various climate areas in the country? Where is adequate water and fertile soil available?"

Next, students might jot down potential comprehension questions: "What is the distribution of crops to available water and soil types? How do crops grown in subtropical areas compare with crops grown in Mediterranean climate areas?"

Continuing on, students might record application questions: "If I were to locate a truck farm, where might I place it? Would I find few tropical crops in the southeast area of the country?"

Possible questions at the analysis level could be: "Are particular crops grown in an area because of climate limitations or because of human

162

preference for particular crops? What particulars are important to consider in analyzing the location of crops and the transportation network?"

The next level of question mapping would be synthesis. Here students investigating this topic might record questions such as: "What statement can I make regarding the use of agricultural resources with Australia? How can I explain the fact that Australia is self-sufficient in food production when so little of the total land area is involved in raising crops?"

The final level mapped is evaluation. Are the general responses to the questions at the synthesis level valid in light of the information processed? Students might also ask, "Are the Australians making wise use of their agricultural resources?" Recorded on a map, the questions indicate to students how to proceed. The map appears in Figure 8-1.

Figure 8-1. Question Map

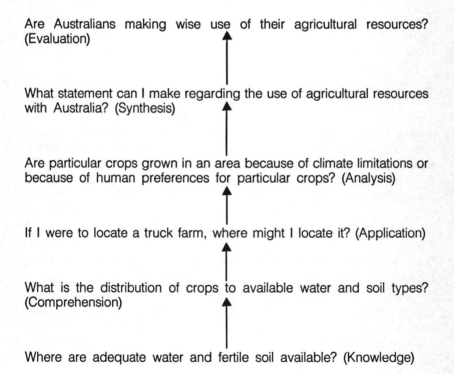

Are Australians making wise use of their agricultural resources? (Evaluation)

What statement can I make regarding the use of agricultural resources with Australia? (Synthesis)

Are particular crops grown in an area because of climate limitations or because of human preferences for particular crops? (Analysis)

If I were to locate a truck farm, where might I locate it? (Application)

What is the distribution of crops to available water and soil types? (Comprehension)

Where are adequate water and fertile soil available? (Knowledge)

VAIL Questioning Strategy

The VAIL Questioning Strategy evolved from investigations of the mental operations of question answering. Its name derives from an investigator's centering on the Verification of the Assertions and Implications of Language (Singer 1981). While the model does not specify the types of questions students should employ at each step of the strategy, they are implied. Students can use questions classified according to Bloom (1956) or some other question classification scheme. The steps of a modified VAIL strategy are (1) question encoding, (2) assessing appropriate information, (3) case interrogation-comparison, and (4) response (Singer 1986).

The strategy is made clear with an example. Assume that in a language arts lesson a student is faced with the following narrative:

The artist painted the picture. The teacher painted the room. The picture was painted with a brush.

Assume further that the student is asked, "Was the picture painted by the artist?" Before responding to the question, the student is instructed to arrange the narrative as points a, b, and c. Now the narrative looks like the following:

a. The artist painted the picture.
b. The teacher painted the room.
c. The picture was painted with a brush.

Arranging the narrative as points a, b, and c will help the student keep track of the various key points of the narrative. While this may seem unnecessary, its value becomes evident if a narrative has many sentences, and the student wishes to identify relationships between and among the sentence statements.

The student employs the strategy in the following manner:

1. *Question Encoding:* In question encoding, the student realizes that questions are verbal packages consisting of one or more propositions (Kintsch 1974). Each proposition contains a predicate and one or more arguments. The predicate incorporates the primary verbal element in a clause. The nouns in the clause are the arguments. Nouns denote agents and patients. The agent is the individual or thing that has executed the action; the patient refers to that person or thing receiving the action.

In responding to the question, "Was the picture painted by the artist?" the student would encode the question as follows: (paint/predi-

164

cate/, agent; artist, patient; picture). In this example, the student is asked to inquire about one particular concept, the artist. In encoding the question, the student strives to distinguish between information given and new information suggested by the question. In our sample narrative, information given is that someone painted the picture. The new information is the request to ascertain if that someone is the artist. Before reading the question, the student really does not know what the purpose of the reading is. The question now makes that clear—the student is to process the narrative to determine if an artist painted the picture. Now that the student is clear as to what the question is and its focus, the students can turn to the second stage of the strategy, assessing the appropriate information. It is obvious that students are not going to pick up question encoding on their own; they will need direct instruction or guided inquiry into the nature and component parts of a question.

2. *Assessing the appropriate information:* At this stage, the student matches the information presented in the question "painted by artist" with either information contained in memory or in the narrative just read. Essentially, the student at this point retrieves from memory the relevant data. "Do artists paint pictures?" Was there anything in the narrative about artists?

3. *Case interrogation-comparison:* In our question, "Was the picture painted by the artist?" the artist is the agent case, the doer of the action. The question has introduced what is demanded of the reader—to find out whether the artist painted the picture. The student now would ask whether or not the previous narrative included any statements about agents; statements (a) and (b) do. But which agent addresses the question?

The student compares the new element, information, of the question, "artist," with information presented in the narrative. Is there any information in the narrative about artist? In our example, there is in statement (a), thus there is a match. The student now can go to the final step in the strategy, creating a response.

4. *Response:* The response is the output of the student's action. Since the student would find in the example a match between element *artist* in the question and the agent *artist* in statement (a), the student can reply yes to the question. "Yes, the picture was painted by the artist." Of course, if the question had been, "Did anyone else paint a picture?" the student, using the same steps, would have responded no.

Students, if they realize that there are various types of questions they

165

can raise to process each step, will engage in these steps with greater skill. For instance, in question encoding, students knowledgeable with comprehension questions will have a fairly easy time identifying predicates and arguments (nouns). They will be able to process the information in the narrative. They will be able to ask themselves what they understand about the statements and what do the statements mean with regard to information brought to the reading. Students need to realize that they will have to ask evaluation questions to determine if information considered in the narrative is appropriate, given the question. Students also must be able to use the skill of the criterion problem.

Case interrogation-comparison requires students to ask analysis questions centering on analysis of elements. Does the information in the narrative present any information that will match the new information in the question? One also has to determine what information is relevant to the question. This requires asking analysis questions. Students at this stage in the strategy may need to ask themselves what information sources are available for researching this question. While there was information on a teacher (agent) painting a room, it was not useful for the question asked that introduced new information—"picture painted by artist?"

The response stage essentially requires students to ask of themselves synthesis questions. What is my response to the question or what is my conclusion to the question based on my reading? Here students must ask questions that enable them to put together the "bits" of information read and then create an answer.

The strategy is graphically presented in Figure 8-2.

Questioning Circle Strategy

The previous strategies discussed are essentially sequential and suggest a hierarchy. An individual using them would employ increasingly higher-level questions. Christenbury and Kelly (1983) presented what they claim is an alternative to sequential and hierarchical questioning strategies. They contend that questions can be grouped in the form of overlapping circles representing different areas or foci of concern. These questions can be asked in various sequences. The three key circles represent major areas about which questions can be asked: (1) the matter, (2) personal reality, and (3) external reality. The first circle area,

Figure 8-2. VAIL Strategy

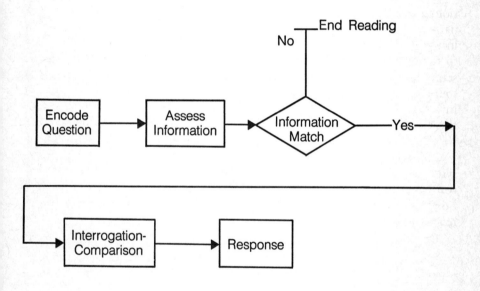

SOURCE: From "Mental Processes of Question Answering," by M.Singer, in *The Psychology of Questions* (p. 143), edited by Arthur C. Graesser and John B. Black, 1986, Hillsdale, N.J.: Lawrence Erlbaum Associates, Inc. Copyright 1986 by Lawrence Erlbaum Associates, Inc. Adapted by permission.

the *matter*, refers to the subject of discussion or questioning. The second circle, *personal reality*, deals with the individual's experiences, values, and ideas. The third circle, *external reality*, refers to the world external to the individual. It subsumes the experience, history, and concepts of other situations, peoples, and cultures.

The questioning circle is depicted in Figure 8-3.

Figure 8-3. Questioning Circle

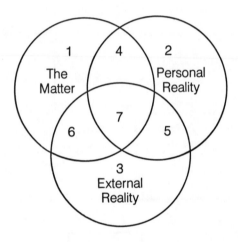

SOURCE: *Questioning, A Path to Critical Thinking*, by L. Christenbury and P. P. Kelly (Urbana, Ill.: ERIC Clearinghouse on Reading and Communication Skills, 1983). Funded by National Institute of Education, U.S. Department of Education.

The questioning circle strategy really presents those realms about which questions can be raised. It also shows when realms can be combined. While the authors present their strategy as an alternative to sequential strategies, it does seem logical that one would always start with the matter—that is, the subject about which one wished to raise questions. The questioning circle does not denote the specific cognitive types of questions that could be asked within each circle area, but the question types are implied. For instance, a student can raise knowledge questions about the matter—questions about facts presented in the material. The student might also raise questions aimed at analyzing or evaluating the matter. To be really skilled questioners, competent performers, students need to know both the questioning strategy and types of possible questions appropriate to their purposes in a given situation.

In presenting this questioning circle strategy to students, it is pointed out that questions, in addition to being raised in the three separate circles should also focus on the intersecting circles, 4, 5, 6, and 7. Further, students should be informed that what the three main circles are called depends on the subject area under investigation. For instance, in a science lesson, the matter may be a particular concept being investigated, such as energy. The personal reality would be that of the student's experiences with the concept, and the external reality would be authorities' views of energy and various scientific laws that refer to energy.

A sketch of a social studies lesson on the family, having students employ the questioning circle strategy is shown in Figure 8-4. The questions raised are noted as to the number of the circle, as presented in Figure 8-4. This lesson sketch ideally would be done by students as they plan their approach to the lesson material.

The goal in using these questions or in having students map out these questions is to get students to raise and process questions in area 7, the intersection of all three circles. Questions at this juncture really demand that students generate general statements about the family. The focus is on creating generalizable knowledge, generating universal content. In dealing with questions at this level, students come to possess rather complete understanding.

CONCLUSION

Students should be the key questioners in the classroom. To assume this role, students need to be directly taught the nature of the question and questioning. Students need to be taught those skills requisite for the competent processing of information. Taught such "know how," students become skilled managers of their own learning, capable of orchestrating their own investigations.

Figure 8-4. Questioning Circle: Family Lesson

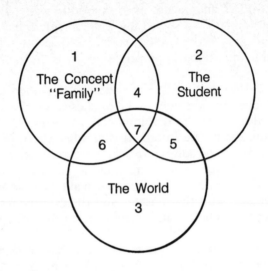

Topic: The Family
Strategy: Questioning Circle
Planning Stage: Question Sketch

Question 1. The Matter: How can we define the term "family"?

Question 2. Personal Reality: Do you live in a family?

Question 3. External Reality: What types of families exist in other nations?

Question 4. The Matter/Personal Reality: Is your family just like the definition of family?

Question 5. Personal Reality/External Reality: In what ways is your family like those in other cultures?

Question 6. The Matter/External Reality: In what ways are the families in other cultures like our definition of family?

Question 7. The Matter/Personal Reality/External Reality: How do you think people have modified the family group to function within their culture context? What general statement or statements can you make about families in the world?

Teaching questioning procedural knowledge, "knowing how," is not done in isolation from declarative knowledge, "knowing that." Rogoff (1982) noted that there is no such thing as pure process. In all learning situations, process learning is tied to content. Students competent in procedural knowledge will possess a richer understanding of declarative knowledge. Students so skilled also should feel more in control of their own learning. Students controlling their learning destinies tend to take joy in learning and to exhibit a desire to truly pursue knowledge. The future requires such individuals.

REFERENCES

Bloom, B. S., et al., eds. *Taxonomy of Educational Objectives: Handbook I. Cognitive Domain*. New York: David McKay, 1956.

Christenbury, L., and Kelly, P. P. *Questioning, A Path to Critical Thinking*. Urbana, Ill.: ERIC Clearinghouse on Reading and Communication Skills, National Council of Teachers of English, 1983.

Dillon, J. T. "Questioning." In *A Handbook of Communication Skills*, edited by Owen Hargie, pp. 95-127. London: Croom Helm, 1986.

————. *Teaching and the Art of Questioning*. Bloomington, Ind.: Phi Delta Kappan Educational Foundation, 1983.

Gavelek, J. R., and Raphael, T. E. "Metacognition, Instruction, and the Role of Questioning Activities." In *Metacognition, Cognition, and Human Performance*, edited by D. L. Forrest-Pressley, G. E. MacKinnon, and T. Gary Waller. Vol. 2, pp. 103-36. Orlando, Fla.: Academic Press, 1985.

Hunkins, F. P. *Involving Students in Questioning*. Boston: Allyn and Bacon, 1976, pp. 11-12.

Hyman, R. T. *Strategic Questioning*. Englewoods Cliffs, N.J.: Prentice-Hall, 1979.

Kintsch, W. *The Representation of Meaning in Memory*. Hillsdale, N.J.: Erlbaum, 1974.

Krathwohl, D. R. *Taxonomy of Educational Objectives, Handbook II, The Affective Domain*. New York: David McKay, 1964.

Miyake, N., and Norman, D. A. "To Ask a Question One Must Know Enough to Know What Is Not Known." *Journal of Verbal Learning and Verbal Behavior* 18 (1979): 351-64.

Postman, N., and Weingartner, C. *Teaching as a Subversive Activity*. New York: Delacorte Press, 1969, p. 23.

Rogers, C. R. *Client-Centered Therapy*. Boston: Houghton Mifflin, 1951.

Rogoff, B. "Integrating Context and Cognitive Development." In *Advances in Developmental Psychology*, edited by M. E. Lamb and A. L. Brown. Vol. 2. Hillsdale, N.J.: Erlbaum, 1982.

Singer, M. "Active Comprehension: From Answering to Asking Questions." *The Reading Teacher* 30 (1978): 901-8.

_____. "Mental Processes of Question Answering." In *The Psychology of Questions*, edited by Arthur C. Graesser and John B. Black. Hillsdale, N.J.: Erlbaum, 1986, pp. 121-56.

_____. "Verifying the Assertions and Implications of Language." *Journal of Verbal Learning and Verbal Behavior* 20 (1981): 46-60.

9. IMPROVING TEACHERS' QUESTIONS AND QUESTIONING: RESEARCH INFORMS PRACTICE

by William W. Wilen, Associate Professor of Education, Department of Teacher Development and Curriculum Studies, Kent State University, Ohio

Consultants: Virginia Atwood, Professor of Education, University of Kentucky, Lexington; and Hans Gerhard Klinzing, University of Tübingen, West Germany

Research has demonstrated that a variety of instructional improvement techniques can be effectively applied in the training of preservice and inservice teachers' questioning skills. Categorized according to four major teacher education training practices (observation, demonstration, practice, and feedback), the following instructional improvement techniques are explored: use of observation instruments, peer observation, instructor modeling, microteaching, minicourses, coaching, self-instruction, self- and shared-analyses of feedback, and objective feedback from students. An observation form is provided to collect data on the cognitive levels of questions and questioning techniques. Implications for implementing the instructional improvement techniques are presented.

As students are leaving his second-period American government class, Mr. Dilling, a twelfth-grade teacher in his fifth year at a suburban school, cannot help but wonder if his teaching efforts are a waste of time for the students and himself. He feels frustrated that his attempts at stimulating discussion on a major current social issue have failed

173

miserably. Only a handful of his thirty students participated and their responses to his questions were considerably less than insightful. The rest of the class was bored and restless. Compounding the problem is the feeling that his inability to be effective seems to be developing into a regular occurrence. Mr. Dilling wonders why the situation has deteriorated and what he can do differently, if anything, to stimulate student thinking and involvement.

A similar experience might occur to a teacher education student on a field experience visit for a methods course. She is asked by her host teacher to review the major facts and concepts from a film the class has just viewed. After her failure to get students to respond to her questions, she wondered if she should stay in teacher education. Nor does this type of episode happen only at the senior high school level; it is just as likely to occur at the elementary or junior high school levels, and in many subject areas. The point is that this situation is not atypical; many teachers need and want assistance in involving their students in thoughtful, lively group interaction.

The responsibility for planning, conducting, and evaluating discussions naturally resides with the teacher. Although many variables within the classroom setting certainly influence the effectiveness of large- and small-group discussions, recitations, and other forms of group interaction, success or failure of such efforts can often be attributed to the teacher's communication skills, particularly the use of questions and questioning techniques. In an analysis of experienced teachers' secondary-level classroom discussions, researchers concluded that the discussions did not achieve their goals because the teachers lacked the necessary skills. Klinzing and Klinzing-Eurich's (1987) primary criticism was that although a variety of thinking levels were stimulated, more indirect discussion techniques were needed to stimulate student involvement. They felt that teachers' probing questions would have served to increase the depth of student responses, and that redirection of questions would have encouraged student-student interaction. Francis (1987) concluded that the teacher-dominated leadership style reduced opportunities for student interaction. These deficiencies are more typical than atypical.

Mr. Dilling's frustration with conducting class discussions possibly can be attributed to a lack of the discussion skills noticed by these researchers. How will what we know about teachers' questions and questioning give Mr. Dilling direction for improvement? The primary purpose of this book has been to provide teachers with a resource on the many facets of questions and questioning. This information is intended to help them make decisions about improving instruction. We know a lot about questions and questioning and are learning more from research each year. Most important for Mr. Dilling, though, is that we know that teachers' questions and questioning techniques directly influence the ways students think and how they interact in the classroom. We also know that teachers can be effectively trained to change their questioning behaviors (Wilen 1986). How can beginning and experienced teachers develop and upgrade questioning skills? What kind of skill development program is most conducive to providing the questioning skills necessary to conduct effective classroom interaction? The purpose of this chapter is to review the literature and research related to a variety of instructional improvement approaches and techniques that are particularly appropriate for developing questioning skills and to propose implications for practice.

INSTRUCTIONAL IMPROVEMENT PRACTICES

A variety of instructional improvement techniques can be effectively applied in the development and training of preservice and inservice teachers' questioning skills. According to a current and comprehensive research review of teacher education training practices conducted by Wade (1985), with support from several other reviews (Broyles and Tillman 1985; Gall et al. 1982; Lanier and Little 1986), the most effective teacher education training programs incorporate the following practices: observation of teaching (both live and simulated), instructor demonstration of skills, practice of skills in simulated and classroom settings, and provision of feedback about performance. The techniques presented in this chapter will be useful to teachers engaging in self-improvement programs, supervisors working with beginning and inservice teachers or conducting workshops on questions and questioning, and college instructors training preservice education students and inservice teachers in questioning skills.

The instructional improvement techniques presented are categorized according to the four major inservice practices noted above. As might be expected, considerable overlapping of the techniques occurs in terms of their primary intent. For example, although microteaching is primarily intended as a technique to provide teachers with opportunities to practice and develop skills, it also provides the opportunity for developing and improving the ability to analyze instruction. The techniques presented are the use of instruments to observe and analyze teaching, peer observation of teaching, instructor modeling of behaviors and skills, microteaching, minicourses, coaching to assist in the transfer of skills to the classroom, self-instruction using training modules, self- and shared-feedback and analysis, and objective feedback from students. In addition, several instructional improvement materials helpful in the development of questioning skills are described.

OBSERVATION OF TEACHING

Observation Instruments

One of the first steps in the instructional improvement process is to gather data on current behavior and skills as displayed in the classroom setting. Most of our observations of our own teaching via audiotape recordings, for example, and our colleagues' teaching, are relatively informal and evaluative. Systematically conducted observations, on the other hand, are descriptive and formal and yield specific data to help in the analysis of teaching. The relatively objective information yielded from systematic observation is useful when making decisions about changing behaviors or techniques. Most observation instruments are tallysheets or checklists of one form or another. They can be used to record data such as the cognitive level of questions asked by a teacher and students, the frequency of such behaviors as the redirection of questions and the use of wait time, and the sequence of questions and techniques such as the use of probing after students' responses. These data-gathering instruments can be used by any observer who has been trained or is familiar with the descriptive categories comprising the form. In the case of self-analysis, the forms can be used in conjunction with an audio or video recording of the class session. The result of such an effort is a fairly specific and objective description of the instructional behavior designated for improvement.

There are over 100 different systematic observation instruments for analyzing aspects of teacher and student verbal and nonverbal behaviors in the classroom. The simpler forms focus on a few behaviors while the more complex focus on multiple behaviors (Simon and Boyer 1970). At least 21 instruments have been identified that are useful to classify questions (Riegle 1976). Some are designed for specific subject areas

176

such as social studies (Schreiber 1967), art (Armstrong and Armstrong 1977), reading (Guszak 1967), and science (Blosser 1979). Another approach categorizes the kinds of questions teachers use to develop different kinds of discussions (Roby 1987). One study (Riley 1980) compared the two most recognized and applied systems for classifying the cognitive levels of questions: Gallagher and Aschner's (1963) adaptation of Guilford's (1956) structure of intellect model and Sanders (1966) adaptation of Bloom's (1956) approach to classifying educational objectives. Teacher education students, using self-instructional training modules made greater gains in recognizing and classifying questions and had a more positive attitude toward using the Aschner-Gallagher approach over students using the Sanders approach. An adaptation of these classification systems is described in detail in Chapter 4 of this book.

Data on the cognitive levels of questions can be gathered systematically in any classroom by listing the levels of questions with their abbreviated definitions down the side of a piece of paper. As a teacher is observed conducting interaction through the use of questions in the classroom, or as a teacher observes an audio or videotape, a tally mark is placed beside the appropriate category. Frequencies and percentages for each category are easily computed giving the teacher an objective accounting of the levels of thinking intended to be stimulated by his or her questions. If data about question sequence are important in the information gathered, consecutive numbers can be used instead of tally marks as questions are coded.

Objective information can also be gathered on the questioning techniques a teacher employs to stimulate thinking and involvement by designing another form of systematic observation. A seating chart with students' names can be used in conjunction with a code to identify various techniques commonly applied in the classroom setting. For example, five of the most common techniques can be given easily identifiable codes:

probing (P): followup to a teacher's question intended to encourage the student to clarify the response, extend thinking or support an opinion;

wait time (WT): pause between the time the teacher has asked a question and a student responds (include number of seconds of wait time used);

participation (V=volunteer and NV=nonvolunteer): balancing the contributions of volunteering and nonvolunteering students;

redirection (R): questions redirected to other students to stimulate involvement and student-student interaction; and

student questions (SQ): questions encouraged by teachers and initiated by students.

Extended commentary on each of these questioning skills and others can be found in Chapter 6 of this book.

As the teacher engages the students in interaction, the observer, or teacher viewing himself or herself on the videotape, codes the symbol corresponding to the appropriate technique on the seating chart at the student's name. For example, a volunteering student who was called on by a teacher to respond to a question after 3 seconds of wait time, would have a "V" and "WT3" by his or her name. If, after an initial response, the teacher probed this student's response to extend thinking, a "P" would then be placed by the name. The completed observation form would give a teacher an objective description of the extent questioning techniques were used with specific students during a discussion or recitation. See Figures 9-1 and 9-2 for an example of an observation form useful to collect data on the cognitive levels of questions based on the Gallagher-Aschner levels (1963) and on teachers' questioning techniques.

Peer Observation

Another instructional improvement technique that has been found to be effective in bringing about changes in teachers' questioning behaviors is peer observation and analysis of teaching. Although peer observation has been used extensively in conjunction with microteaching at the preservice level, it has become increasingly effective in inservice education.

One of the most successful inservice programs that heavily involves the use of peer observation and analysis is the Teacher Expectations and Student Achievement (TESA) Program developed by Kerman (1979). TESA is designed to encourage teachers to use nondiscriminatory behavior toward all students to increase their academic performance. Five workshops are conducted to train teachers to develop skill in using 15 specific behaviors, organized into five units, several of which focus on questioning techniques; latency (wait time), delving (probing and prompting), and higher-level questioning (questions above the knowledge level). After each workshop training session, each teacher practices the skills in his or her own classroom with peers from their small team observing individually for 30 minutes. The demonstration teacher, in turn, also observes team peers practicing the skills. Data are gathered by the peers using systematic observation instruments that identify the frequency with which the teacher directs each of the unit skills to identified high- and low-ability students. The instruments are left with the demonstration teacher for self-analysis. Further reflection and shared-analysis take place during the next workshop session.

The effectiveness of using peer observation as a means to assist in the training of teachers was demonstrated in a study by Sparks (1984). Junior high school teachers of low-achieving students were trained in several effective teaching techniques. The teachers were divided into three workshop groups: workshop only, workshop plus peer observation, and workshop plus coaching, which is trainer-provided direct assistance to the teachers in their classroom situations. It was found that the teachers made significant changes in their teaching behaviors and that peer observation was the most effective means.

INSTRUCTOR DEMONSTRATION OF SKILLS

Modeling

One of the most influential instructional techniques is modeling through the use of demonstration. Modeling is an essential component of the minicourse approach used to train teachers in asking higher-level questions and in using a variety of questioning skills. A major body of research on modeling comes from the area of social learning theory. Based on his review of research, much of which he has conducted, Bandura (1969) concluded that people learn simply from observing the behaviors of knowledgeable and skillful models.

A teacher's use of demonstrations to enhance students' learning is the most direct use of modeling as a teaching device. Based on their review of the research, Good and Brophy (1984) proposed a sequence of steps for an effective demonstration that can be directly applied when teaching questioning skills to preservice and inservice teachers. The procedure involves providing an overview and rationale for the skill,

179

Figure 9-1. Cognitive Questions and Questioning Observation Form

Teacher's Name: _Kathy W._   Date: _1/9/87_

Observer's Name: _Charles N._   Period/Time: _3d_

Rationale: Used during interactive sessions such as discussion and recitation for the primary purpose of determining the levels of student thinking stimulated and the extent questioning techniques are being employed. The seating arrangement provided on this form should be modified to suit the instructional situation. This traditional arrangement is more appropriate for a recitation than a discussion.

QUESTION LEVELS:

	Number of questions asked	Percent of total
I. *Cognitive-Memory:* narrow, closed questions that require students to recall or recognize information. Students recall, recognize, define, repeat, quote, identify, or answer yes or no.	~~HH~~ III 8	53
II. *Convergent:* narrow questions that require students to combine and analyze remembered information. Students translate, interpret, relate, explain, compare, contrast, analyze, associate, conclude, summarize, or reason.	IIII 4	27
III. *Divergent:* broad, open-ended questions that require students to develop their own information or to view a topic from a new perspective. Students hypothesize, speculate, devise, infer, predict, imply, synthesize, or solve lifelike problems.	I 1	7
IV. *Evaluative:* broad, open-ended questions that require students to judge, value, or choose with support from internal or external sources. Students opine, judge, rate, or make a choice.	II 2	13

Class Front

P: probing as a followup to clarify, extend, or support thinking

WT_: wait time after a question before student response (include number of seconds)

V or NV: volunteering or nonvolunteering student called upon

R: redirection of question to another student

SQ: student question initiated by the student or solicited by the teacher

Andrew	Emily	Claire	Erik	Chris	Leslie
VWT_3	SQ		R		VWT_2 VWT_3 PP

Eric	John	Aaron	Kristin	Jason	Anna
	VWT_3	VWT_3 VWT_2 PSQ		NV PP	R

Ed	Laurie	Jeremy	Paul	Rachael	Amy
			NV		

Laura	Jennifer	Rick	Theresa	Harry	Michael
	VWT_3 VWT_3	VWT_3			

Ann	Shelly	Sarah	Elizabeth		Molly
			VWT_3 P		

Figure 9-2. Cognitive Questions and Questioning Observation Form

Teacher's Name: _____ Date: _____

Observer's Name: _____ Period/Time: _____

Rationale: Used during interactive sessions such as discussion and recitation for the primary purpose of determining the levels of student thinking stimulated and the extent questioning techniques are being employed. The seating arrangement provided on this form should be modified to suit the instructional situation. This traditional arrangement is more appropriate for a recitation than a discussion.

	Number of questions asked	Percent of total

QUESTION LEVELS:

I. *Cognitive-Memory:* narrow, closed questions that require students to recall or recognize information. Students recall, recognize, define, repeat, quote, identify, or answer yes or no.

_____ _____

II. *Convergent:* narrow questions that require students to combine and analyze remembered information. Students translate, interpret, relate, explain, compare, contrast, analyze, associate, conclude, summarize, or reason.

_____ _____

III. *Divergent:* broad, open-ended questions that require students to develop their own information or to view a topic from a new perspective. Students hypothesize, speculate, devise, infer, predict, imply, synthesize, or solve lifelike problems.

_____ _____

IV. *Evaluative:* broad, open-ended questions that require students to judge, value, or choose with support from internal or external sources. Students opine, judge, rate, or make a choice.

_____ _____

Class Front

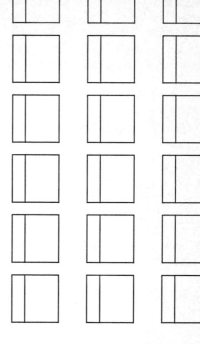

QUESTIONING TECHNIQUES:

P: probing as a followup to clarify, extend, or support thinking

WT__: wait time after a question before student response (include number of seconds)

V or NV: volunteering or nonvolunteering student called upon

R: redirection of question to another student

SQ: student question initiated by the student or solicited by the teacher demonstrating and explaining the skill step-by-step, performing it in "slow motion," having trainees practice the skill while being observed and receiving corrective feedback, and correcting mistakes.

In a study designed to identify an approach to train preservice teachers in wait time, DeTure (1979) found modeling to be efficient and effective. The group of preservice elementary teachers who were trained with video models extended their wait time over audio model groups. Wait time 2, or the pause after a student has responded, was found to be the most affected, increasing from 0.60 seconds during the pretest to 2.32 seconds after the video modeling treatment.

PRACTICE OF SKILLS

Microteaching

Microteaching is a training approach involving scaled-down teaching for the purpose of developing and practicing specific teaching skills. As it was originally conceived, preservice teachers taught brief (5- to 10-minute) lessons to small groups (four to five) of pupils demonstrating a specific skill that they have been taught. Some of the original microteaching skills focused on fluency in asking questions, probing questions, higher-order questions, and divergent questions. The lessons were videotaped and the followup consisted of the teacher education student and the instructor analyzing and evaluating the performance for the purpose of further skill development and improvement. The lesson was then repeated with another group of pupils (Allen and Ryan 1969).

Today, microteaching is also used with inservice teachers and training involves teaching peers who sometimes role play pupils at a particular grade level. Its value as an instructional method to develop competence is that it permits preservice and inservice teachers to test and practice discrete teaching skills within the relatively safe environment of a simulated classroom with peers. Most important, immediate feedback about one's performance is available through viewing the tape and discussion with instructor and peers.

The research on microteaching generally supports its effectiveness as an instructional technique to develop and improve teachers' questions and questioning techniques. In a study reported by Walberg (1986), microteaching was found to have substantial effects on the development of teacher education students' instructional skills, including questioning,

184

at the elementary and secondary levels (Butcher 1981). Madike (1980) found that student teachers who were trained through microteaching procedures displayed more effective skills, including questioning, and affected their pupils' mathematics achievement more than student teachers who had not been trained through microteaching.

An adaptation of the microteaching training model used in Madike's (1980) study will serve as an illustration of how the procedure can be applied in preservice and inservice settings. A detailed explanation, perhaps with a brief review of current research, is provided to teacher education students or teachers serving as trainees to introduce one specific questioning skill such as student questions. Next a videotape of a teacher, or videotapes of several teachers, effectively encouraging students to formulate and ask questions within the context of the classroom is shown to demonstrate a realistic perspective of the skill in action. The trainees then read about student questioning and specifically how teachers apply the skill as a part of their repertoire of questioning techniques in the classroom on a regular basis. They then practice designing directives and questions that would encourage students to ask questions related to particular subject matter content. The next phase involves the trainees in writing a plan for a 10- to 15-minute lesson during which the skill of student questioning is to be demonstrated. The lesson is then taught to a small group of peers role playing pupils of the age for which the lesson is intended. The lesson is videotaped. Immediately afterwards the trainee views the videotape and performs a self-analysis using a rating form. A conference is held with the instructor for the purpose of comparing assessments of the performance and preparing for a reteach emphasizing improvement in the areas identified. This process is repeated for all of the identified problem areas.

Minicourses

The minicourse approach to instructional improvement specifically aims at changing the classroom behavior of teachers. It was originally designed for use as an inservice program in schools but has also been used as part of preservice training programs. The minicourse approach differs from microteaching in that a minicourse is a self-contained package of training materials. Minicourses provide feedback through a structured self-evaluation of videotaped teaching performance. In contrast, microteaching is an elaborate training procedure involving supervisory feedback. Originally developed at the Far West Laboratory for

Educational Research and Development, two minicourses related to questioning were developed (Minicourses 1 and 9):

Minicourse 1—Effective Questioning: Elementary Level is an inservice program consisting of instructional sequences for intermediate-level teachers focusing on 12 specific questioning behaviors necessary for conducting a discussion. They are:

I. 5-second wait time;
   dealing with incorrect answers acceptingly and nonpunitively;
   balancing volunteering and nonvolunteering students' responses;

II. redirecting questions to several students;
   framing questions to encourage longer student responses;
   framing questions to encourage higher-cognitive-level responses;

III. prompting;
   seeking clarification;
   refocusing students' responses;

IV. not repeating one's own questions;
   not answering one's own questions;
   not repeating students' answers. (Borg, Kelly, and Langer 1970)

Minicourse 9—High Cognitive Questioning focuses on the levels of questions based on Bloom's (1956) taxonomy and is designed to help teachers increase their students' ability to think. The minicourse is presented in four lessons:

I. probing questions;

II. analysis questions;

III. synthesis questions;

IV. evaluation questions.

The Minicourse 9 "package" consists of a teacher handbook, a coordinator handbook and five films (one introductory film, three instructional films, and one model film). The instructional sequence begins with the teacher reading the section of the handbook on a particular level of questions, for example. After viewing the appropriate instructional and model films, the teacher plans a lesson emphasizing stimulating the appropriate level of thinking through questions to be

186

taught to a small group of pupils. After the microteaching, the videotape is viewed and evaluated. The lesson is replanned to take into account improvements and the lesson is retaught to another group of pupils. The retaught lesson is viewed and evaluated again, thus completing the instructional cycle (Gall, Dunning, and Weathersby 1971).

Use of the minicourses as training tools is very effective in preservice and inservice situations. In one study comparing Minicourse 1—Effective Questioning with the microteaching training approach combined with student teaching, Borg, Kallenbach, and Friebel (1968) found the minicourse approach to be more effective in changing the questioning behaviors of student teachers than student teaching alone. Buttery (1978) found similar results in his study using a modified approach to Minicourse 1. Teachers' classrooms were used rather than microteaching labs, thereby eliminating the use of videotape equipment. Also using Minicourse 1 to train student and cooperating teachers, Pagliaro (1978) found that student teachers increased their frequency of questioning behaviors when placed with cooperating teachers who used high frequencies of questioning behaviors. In another study, this time using Minicourse 9—High Cognitive Questioning, Malvern (1980) found the comprehension skills of pupils of teachers trained using the minicourse approach improved over the skills of pupils of teachers who had not taken the minicourse.

Minicourse 9 was translated and adapted for preservice and inservice teacher training at the Center for New Learning Methods, University of Tübingen, West Germany. Further, it was field-tested in elementary and secondary schools. Results of the studies (Klinzing-Eurich and Klinzing 1980) indicated that elementary teachers increased their use of higher-cognitive-level and probing questions in classroom discussions, and the changes persisted three months later. Secondary teacher education students increased the percentage of higher cognitive questions but not their probing questions. Another finding was that student behavior changed considerably. The percentage of pupil talk and pupil initiated comments and questions, and the length and frequency of higher cognitive comments and questions of elementary and secondary students increased. A recent reanalysis of the data of these studies also revealed a significant increase in the proportion of correspondences between the cognitive levels of teachers' questions and students' responses (Klinzing, Klinzing-Eurich, and Tisher 1985). The adaptation of the minicourse to the teacher training system of West Germany has been quite successful.

Coaching

The training component of coaching has also been demonstrated as an effective approach to assist teachers to transfer newly learned instructional skills to classroom practice. The rationale for involving a coach such as a peer, supervisor, principal, or college instructor to assist in the implementation and practice of a new skill in the classroom is that the process of skill transfer is more involved than previously perceived. This is particularly the case with complex skills because of the difficulty of integrating them into a teacher's existing repertoire. The procedure of coaching consists of giving encouragement and support, providing technical assistance and feedback, and assisting in deciding when it is appropriate to apply the skill. Studies support coaching as an effective training component (Showers 1983; Joyce 1986).

Self-Instruction

The process of self-instructional improvement can be implemented in numerous ways ranging from informal to formal. Although most teachers approach self-improvement informally, almost casually, because it is convenient, nonthreatening, and inexpensive, it is also the least effective in changing instructional behavior. In contrast, a formal approach to self-improvement is structured in terms of the extent of time devoted to the process, objectivity of data collection and analysis, and systematic nature of engaging in the training activities.

One of the most effective forms of self-training leading to improvement in the area of questions and questioning is use of the self-instructional module. At the preservice level, Merwin and Schneider (1973) successfully used self-instructional modules to train secondary-level social studies student teachers to plan, question, and test for higher-level thinking. The experimental group achieved higher achievement test scores and student teaching performance ratings than the control group, which was taught questioning skills using conventional teaching practices including lecture, discussion, demonstration, and microteaching. Also attempting to improve teachers' ability to ask higher-level questions, Zoch (1971) employed an individualized inservice approach with experimental and control groups of kindergarten and first-grade teachers. The individualized approach significantly improved teachers' ability to ask higher-level questions but did not make a difference in the amount of verbal interaction stimulated.

Several individualized inservice training packets designed to develop

188

skill in asking questions at a variety of cognitive levels and skill in using several questioning techniques have been produced by universities and commercial firms (Licata, Sinatra, and Masia 1977; Lowery and Marshall 1980; McMillan, Burke, and Piece 1970; Holder 1977). These have been developed primarily for use by individual teachers. The components of the packages generally include written or audiotaped procedures, pretest and posttest to measure changes in performance levels, written instructional materials, audiotaped demonstration lessons for skill development, procedures for practicing and systematically analyzing the skills in the classroom using audiotaped recordings of performances, and a bibliography. Most have been field-tested prior to marketing.

FEEDBACK ABOUT PERFORMANCE

Self- and Shared-Feedback and Analysis

One reason why microteaching and minicourses have experienced success as training approaches derives from the self-confrontation dynamic created when a teacher initially views himself or herself on videotape. In their review of the literature, Fuller and Manning (1973) concluded that self-confrontation can increase the accuracy of self-perception and has the potential for increasing teachers' realism about themselves. Of course, receptivity to feedback is a prerequisite to benefiting from feedback.

In order for self-confrontation to be effective and initiate the process of behavioral change, viewing the videotape of one's teaching should be focused and involve another observer in the feedback process. Simply viewing oneself on tape conducting a discussion in the classroom will probably not generate the insight for learning or motivation to change. According to Fuller and Manning (1973), the presence of another observer increases the potential that the focus of the feedback will shift from the physical self to the teaching act. Change involves identifying a discrepancy between one person's view of "reality" and that of another observer. The other observer could be a supervisor formally assisting in his or her role to improve instruction. However, a less threatening observer would be a colleague who has been requested to provide a second point of view. Systematic observation instruments would also be very useful in this feedback process to objectively record and analyze the data related to the designated area.

189

Student Feedback

Another source of feedback that teachers have readily available to provide them with information on questioning behaviors is the students. Support in the literature for involving students is growing. As a result of observing teachers many hours each week, students can be a reliable source of feedback. Furthermore, students provide a large sample as observers, thereby reducing individual biases and increasing reliability. Other advantages of involving students in the analysis of teaching is that the process requires little time and can fit conveniently into the class schedule (Hogg and Wilen 1976).

Essential to using students effectively as a source of objective data about a teacher's questioning behaviors is to train them to use a systematic observation instrument. If the focus is on identifying the cognitive levels of questions a teacher asks in the classroom, several students easily could be trained to identify convergent and divergent questions based on the interpretation by Gallagher and Aschner (1963). The terms "broad" or "open-ended" and "narrow" and "closed" might be used instead of the more formal terms. More capable students might categorize questions based on the Gallagher and Aschner (1963) levels and an instrument can easily be devised based on the design presented earlier in this chapter. The trained students simply place a tally mark in either the convergent or divergent category corresponding to the level of question asked. Hogg and Wilen (1976) provide an example of an instrument that is used to gather sequential information on four cognitive levels and also permits the coding of teacher statements. These additional data are useful in determining the proportion of time the teacher spent providing information and asking for information during a discussion. Students can also conveniently and reliably provide feedback on such questioning techniques as wait time, redirection of questions to other students, and the extent the contributions of volunteering and nonvolunteering students are used. Objective feedback from students can be a valuable source of information on teacher questioning behaviors.

ADDITIONAL RESOURCES

Several other resources might be useful to those involved with training preservice and inservice teachers to develop skills in asking questions and using questioning techniques.

"Questioneze" (Gillin et al. 1972) was designed as a gaming approach to help teachers vary the cognitive levels of their verbal and written questions. The questioning classification scheme used is based on the works of Bloom (1956) and Sanders (1966). Training centers around three games: Taxo—a card game to help teachers practice ordering the Bloom categories; Queskno—a bingo-type game to practice classifying questions; and Quesco—a small-group game to practice composing questions at six cognitive levels. Quesco is particularly useful in training because teachers are applying their knowledge by formulating questions. It is also very competitive and challenging.

The National Education Association (1984) has produced a 10-minute sound filmstrip, *Questioning Techniques, for Teachers and Students*, that is based on a monograph from its What Research Says to the Teacher Series, *Questioning Skills, for Teachers* (Wilen 1986). A transcript of this filmstrip script is presented in the Appendix of this chapter. It provides an overview of the kinds of questions teachers should ask and the techniques they could use to ask them in their classrooms. Involving students in asking questions is also covered. Simulated teaching episodes illustrate the different question levels and techniques.

An electronic feedback device has been created to assist the training of teachers to extend their wait time after a question has been asked and after the student has responded. The Wait Timer is a voice-activated, self-contained, portable device that gives a visual indication of a three-second wait time. Using the device in a research study involving middle school science teachers, Swift and Gooding (1983) found that as teachers increased their wait time, the frequency and quality of students' responses increased.

IMPLICATIONS FOR PRACTICE

As we reflect on the introductory scenario and Mr. Dilling's frustration with conducting discussions, we realize now that the processes and resources for instructional improvement to help him are available. Findings from research over the past 20 years have revealed that preservice and inservice teachers can change their questioning behaviors and become more effective in stimulating interaction in the classroom. Teachers can successfully be trained to raise the cognitive levels of their questions—a necessary and practical way to stimulate students' thinking during discussion. Further, teachers can expand their repertoires of questioning techniques with skills that encourage students to participate in interactive sessions.

There is hope for Mr. Dilling because he has several options available to him if he chooses to investigate why his attempts at stimulating discussions have failed. First, he needs to become aware of the questioning behaviors in which he engages while conducting discussions as well as students' reactions to those behaviors. Research recommends self-confrontation to discover discrepancies between one's impressions of what exists and what actually exists. This will help Mr. Dilling pinpoint possible problems. A videotape, or at least an audiotape, is a useful means of identifying discussion-related behaviors. An alternative, or an approach to use along with making a videotape, is to use the students as a source of information about questioning behaviors. A trusted colleague may be invited to observe the class and/or the videotape to assist with the analysis. Data collection and analysis will be more objective if systematic observation instruments are available or have been created for this important initial stage of the inquiry. Based on the outcomes of this observation, and data gathering and analysis, decisions can be made about those behaviors that need to be investigated further or changed.

At this point, Mr. Dilling could continue the self-improvement instructional process or seek outside assistance from someone in his district or from a nearby college or university. Self-instructional packages for improving questions and questioning are available to facilitate skills development and transfer to the classroom. Another more formal alternative is to identify a course or workshop being conducted that has as its focus, or part of it, skill development in conducting discussions and recitations. Perhaps other secondary and elementary teachers within the district are experiencing similar problems as Mr. Dilling and an inservice program may be arranged focusing on questioning skills. It would be advantageous to contact outside sources such as the state department of education or a nearby university for assistance in developing it. This book, or others that also have reviewed the research and literature on questions and questioning, is also very useful as a resource in planning specific workshop sessions.

Mr. Dilling will benefit greatly if the workshop, course, or inservice program is conducted by a person who has substantial expertise in the area of questions and questioning and who can continually and effectively model and demonstrate the skills during the sessions. The instructor needs to utilize a variety of instructional approaches, particularly during the skill development sessions. Research findings are in agreement that the instructor should build in opportunities for the teachers to observe and analyze the skills being demonstrated live and on videotape, practice the skills in simulated settings using microteaching approaches with peers and/or small groups of pupils, and receive systematic feedback about one's performance. These training components also benefit undergraduate students in teacher education programs.

The instructor should encourage the teachers to apply the skills in their own classrooms with further feedback from colleagues who observe the skills in action. A variation is to build into the skill development sessions the minicourses focusing on developing teachers' higher-cognitive questions and questioning techniques. Ideally, the instructor, whether he or she is a consultant, supervisor, university instructor, or some other trained person, would be able to assist teachers in applying the skills in their classrooms. Mr. Dilling can be assured that an instructional program incorporating these practices and techniques will increase the probability that questioning skills will be developed, their transfer to the classroom will be facilitated, and instruction will be improved.

Striving to become a more effective instructor is an intention associated with committed teachers. Because questioning is an influential teaching act, any improvement in questioning practices is likely to have a marked impact on instructional effectiveness. Therefore, any teacher who has not already done so would by all odds benefit from improved questioning skills. The information presented in this chapter is intended to provide encouragement and direction to any teacher or teacher educator for whom developing and upgrading questioning skills is an area of potential interest.

APPENDIX

QUESTIONING TECHNIQUES, FOR TEACHERS AND STUDENTS
(Filmstrip script based on the work of William W. Wilen*)

1. Music (Title frame)
2. Music (Source)
3. Mr. Lane's sixth graders are discussing a story about runaway children. The topic is of great interest because of a recent local case.
4. First, the teacher asks a shy boy who rarely volunteers, "Tom, how did Joe's parents discover he was missing?"
5. After Tom's reply, Mr. Lane continues, "What were some of the reasons for Joe's running away? ... Anne?"
6. Then, after Anne's response, he asks, "Would anyone like to add another reason? ... How about you, Bill?"
7. Following Bill's reply, the teacher asks, "Do any of the reasons Anne and Bill gave us seem serious enough to make a child run away from home?"
8. Several children wave their hands eagerly and give their replies.
9. Then Mr. Lane goes on, "Why do you think Joe's friends never suspected that he was unhappy enough to run away?"
10. The teacher calls on Kathy after a three-second pause.
11. Kathy's response is rather vague, so the teacher follows it up to get more details and clarity—"Can you mention a few of the clues given in the story?"
12. After several other probing questions, he asks, "If you were a friend of Joe's and knew about his problems, how could you have helped him?"
13. Mr. Lane used several effective questioning techniques in this class discussion.
14. First, he phrased his questions clearly, using content and vocabulary that were familiar to his students.
15. This technique encouraged students' understanding and reduced the possibility of confusion and anxiety.
16. Second, he asked questions at a variety of levels. He started with memory-level questions to check students' knowledge of the story.
17. Then he moved on to more difficult questions so that students could practice higher-level thinking skills that he had been emphasizing in class.
18. Third, he gave students time to think before answering the more difficult questions.
19. Research tells us that teachers who use "wait time"—a pause of 3 to 5 seconds before a student response, especially to higher-level questions—encourage higher-level answers.
20. Fourth, Mr. Lane used probing questions to get students to clarify and extend their thinking. This technique also helped improve students' responses.
21. And, fifth, he called on both volunteers and nonvolunteers. This technique encouraged greater student participation.
22. At the local high school, Ms. Walker's junior class in American history is studying a unit on social issues of the 60's.

---

*For further information, contact the NEA Professional Library, 1201 16th Street, NW, Washington, DC 20036.

23. Ms. Walker has planned a discussion using a sequence of questions to improve her students' thinking and learning skills.

24. She begins with a question on the assigned reading: "According to the author, what were the major social issues of the 60's?"

25. Students must recall information to answer this cognitive-memory-level question.

26. Ms. Walker asks several other similar questions to check students' knowledge about the facts of each issue.

27. Then she asks several convergent questions. These higher-level questions require students to compare and analyze information that they remember.

28. Ms. Walker pauses a full five seconds before calling on Ruben to answer ... "Which issue has had the greatest effect on life in the 80's?"

29. She follows up the boy's response with a probing question: "Can you give some evidence to back up your answer, Ruben?"

30. While Ruben is speaking, several students indicate their disagreement.

31. "Lucy, do you have something to add to Ruben's comments?"

32. At this point the teacher departs from her planned questions to give Lucy and three other students a chance to express their views.

33. Then Ms. Walker continues with a divergent question. To answer this broad, open-ended question, students must expand information they have or look at the topic from a new perspective.

34. "How might the economy have been affected if the United States had not sent troops to Vietnam?"

35. Ms. Walker's final question is evaluative. To answer this broad, open-ended question, students must project and support their judgments, values, and choices.

36. "Which issue do you think will have the most far-reaching effects on the lives of most people in the United States?"

37. As these two episodes illustrate, teachers at different grade levels can improve their instruction with effective questioning techniques.

38. These techniques can have a great influence on student thinking and learning. Research has shown that many of them are directly related to increased academic achievement.

39. Researchers have also found that teachers' questions can control the thought level of students' responses.

40. This means that teacher who ask higher-level questions can expect higher-level answers from students who have had practice with different question levels. On the other hand, it means that teachers who ask lower-level questions can expect students to give lower-level answers.

41. The importance of "wait time"—studied by Mary Budd Rowe—is one of the major research findings about questioning techniques.

42. According to the studies, teachers who pause 3 to 5 seconds after asking a question help students in many ways.

43. For example, with wait time the length and cognitive level of students' answers increase;

44. ... the number of voluntary answers increases;

45. ... students' confidence in responding increases;

46. ... the number of students' questions increases;

47. ... and the number of students who fail to respond decreases.

48. Research also tells us that teachers can improve their questioning levels and techniques with training and practice. The first step is to become aware of your current questioning behaviors.

49. One way to do this is to videotape or tape-record a questioning session in your classroom. Then identify and analyze the questions you used.

50. For example, ... how often did you use cognitive-memory-level questions?

51. ... how often did you use convergent questions?

52. ... divergent questions?

53. ... and how often did you use evaluative questions?

54. Did you phrase your questions at the appropriate cognitive level to achieve your lesson objectives?

55. Did you phrase your questions clearly and adjust them to the language and ability levels of your students?

56. Did you use wait time—especially after higher-level questions—to give students time to think?

57. Did you ask questions for the group and for individuals—to provide a balance?

58. Did you call on nonvolunteers as well as volunteers—to encourage participation?

59. Did you follow up with probing questions to encourage students to complete, clarify, expand, or support their original replies?

60. You might want to use an observation form with the audiotape or videotape to help you gather information on your questioning levels and techniques.

61. To make your own form, just list the question levels and techniques. Then check the number of times you used each level in the lesson. Also rate yourself on how effectively you used each technique.

62. The next step is to plan your lessons to include any changes you need to make.

63. Then tape-record or videotape a second lesson with your students, using these improved questioning techniques.

64. And, once more, identify and analyze your questions for any further changes that may be needed.

65. Repeat this procedure—planning, taping, and analyzing—until you have reached your questioning goals.

66. Another way to stimulate students' involvement and thinking is to encourage students to ask questions.

67. According to research, students ask very few questions in the classroom. They expect to answer questions, not to ask them.

68. Some research also shows that student's questioning skills lead to higher achievement.

69. Teachers who train their students to ask questions can help them to use information more independently.

70. Teachers can encourage students to increase the number and kind of questions they ask by using many strategies.

71. For example, Mr. Vega begins a science fiction unit by asking his ninth graders to write three questions about future scientific possibilities they would like to have answered.

72. The students' enthusiasm grows when they discover they will be looking for answers to their own questions.

73. In addition, the teacher provides opportunities for students to devise their own questions to help them examine and analyze information as they read the assigned material.
74. Then, noting the popularity of Ray Bradbury's stories, Mr. Vega asks, "If Ray Bradbury were here today, which one question would each of you like to ask him?"
75. Finally, the teacher has students rank-order all the questions according to their interest, and send the top five questions to the science fiction writer requesting his response.
76. Teachers can improve communication and learning in the classroom by improving their own questioning skills and by helping students to develop theirs.
77. More specifically, teachers can help their students develop their ability to think critically and creatively—a major goal of instruction.
78. Remember—"To question well is to teach well."
79. Music (Credit frame)
80. Music (Copyright)

REFERENCES

Allen, D., and Ryan, Kevin. *Microteaching*. Reading, Mass.: Addison-Wesley, 1969.

Armstrong, C. L., and Armstrong, N. A. "Art Teacher Questioning Strategy." *Studies in Art Education* 18 (1977): 53-64.

Bandura, A. (1969). *Principles of Behavior Modification*. New York: Holt, Rinehart and Winston, 1969.

Bloom, B. S., et al., eds. *Taxonomy of Educational Objectives: Handbook I. Cognitive Domain*. New York: David McKay, 1956.

Blosser, P. E. *Review of Research: Teacher Questioning Behavior in Science Classrooms*. Columbus, Ohio: ERIC Information Analysis Center for Science, Mathematics and Environmental Education, 1979. ERIC Document ED 184 818.

Borg, W. R.; Kallenbach, M. M.; and Friebel, A. "The Effects of Videotape Feedback and Microteaching in a Teacher Training Model." Berkeley, Calif.: Far West Laboratory for Educational Research and Development, 1968.

Borg, W. R.; Kelley, M. L; and Langer, P. *Minicourse 1: Effective Questioning. Elementary Level*. Far West Laboratory for Educational Research and Development. New York: Macmillan, 1970.

Broyles, I., and Tillman, M. "Relationships of Inservice Training Components and Changes in Teacher Concerns Regarding Innovations." *Journal of Educational Research* 78 (1985): 364-71.

Butcher, P. M. "An Experimental Investigation of the Effectiveness of a Value Strategy Unit for Use in Teacher Education." Ph.D. diss., Macquarie University, Sydney, Australia, 1981.

Buttery, T. J., and Michalak, D. A. "Modifying Questioning Behavior via the Teaching Clinic Process. *Educational Research Quarterly* 3 (1978): 46-56.

DeTure, L. R. "Relative Effects of Modeling in the Acquisition of Wait Time by Preservice Elementary Teachers and Concomitant Changes in Dialogue Patterns. *Journal of Research in Science Teaching* 16 (November 1979): 553-62.

Francis, E. "Group Processes." In *Questioning and Discussion: A Multidisciplinary Study*, edited by J. T. Dillon. Norwood, N.J.: Ablex Publishing, 1987.

Fuller, F., and Manning, B. "Self-Confrontation Reviewed: A Conceptualization for Video Playback in Teacher Education." *Review of Educational Research* 43 (1973): 469-528.

Gall, M. D.; Dunning, B.; and Weathersby, R. *Minicourse 9: Higher Cognitive Questioning*. Far West Laboratory for Educational Research and Development. New York: Macmillan, 1971.

Gall, M. D.; Haisley, F. B.; Baker, R. G.; and Perez, M. (1982). *The Relationship Between Inservice Education Practices and Effectiveness of Basic Skills Instruction. Final Report*. Eugene, Ore.: University of Oregon Center for Educational Policy and Management, 1982. ERIC Document ED 228 745.

Gallagher, J. J., and Aschner, M. J. "A Preliminary Report on the Analysis of Classroom Interaction." *Merrill-Palmer Quarterly* 9 (1963): 183-95.

Gillin, C. J; Kysilka, M. L.; Rogers, V.; and Smith, L. *Questioneze. Individual or Group Game Involvement for Developing Questioning Skills*. Columbus, Ohio: Charles E. Merrill, 1972.

Good, T. L., and Brophy, J. E. *Looking in Classrooms*. 3d ed. New York: Harper and Row, 1984.

Guilford, J. P. "The Structure of Intellect." *Psychological Bulletin* 53 (July 1956): 267-93.

Guszak, F. J. "Teacher Questioning and Reading." *The Reading Teacher* 21 (1967); 227-34.

Hogg, J. H., and Wilen, W. W. "Evaluating Teachers' Questions: A New Dimension in Students' Assessment of Instruction." *Phi Delta Kappan* 58 (November 1976): 281-82.

Holder, L. E. (1977). *Questioning That Turns Students On Rather Than Off. Description of Teacher Inservice Education Materials*. Washington, D.C.: National Education Association, 1977. ERIC Document ED 171 685.

Joyce, B. *Improving America's Schools*. New York: Longman, 1986.

Kerman, S. "Teacher Expectations and Student Achievement." *Phi Delta Kappan* 60 (June 1979): 716-18.

Klinzing, H. G. and Klinzing-Eurich, G. "Questions, Responses and Reactions." In *Questioning and Discussion: A Multidisciplinary Study*, edited by J. T. Dillon. Norwood, N.J.: Ablex Publishing, 1987.

Klinzing, H. G.; Klinzing-Eurich, G.; and Tisher, R. P. "Higher Cognitive Behaviors in Classroom Discourse: Congruencies Between Teachers' Questions and Pupils' Responses." *Australian Journal of Education* 29 (1985): 63-75.

Klinzing-Eurich, G., and Klinzing, H. G. "Adaptation of Evaluation of Minicourses in West Germany." Paper presented at the American Educational Research Association Annual Meeting, Boston, 1980.

Lanier, J. E., and Little, J. W. "Research on Teacher Education." In *Handbook of Research on Teaching*, edited by M. C. Wittrock. 3d ed. New York: Macmillan, 1986.

Licata, W.; Sinatra, L.; and Masia, J. (1977). *The Use of Higher Level Questions (Module 2). Description of Teacher Education Inservice Materials.* Washington, D.C.: National Education Association, 1977. ERIC Document ED 169 002.

Lowery, L. F., and Marshall, H. H. *Learning About Instruction: Teacher-Initiated Verbal Directions and Eliciting Questions. A Personal Workshop.* Berkeley, Calif.: University of California Professional Development and Applied Research Center, 1980. ERIC Document ED 246 012.

McMillan, B.; Burke, R.; and Piece, E. *Questioning Skills (Cluster V; 5 Modules—A Summary). Description of Teacher Inservice Education Materials.* Washington, D.C.: National Education Association, May 1970. ERIC Document ED 169 064.

Madike, F. U. "Teacher Classroom Behaviors Involved in Microteaching and Student Achievement: A Regression Study." *Journal of Educational Psychology* 72 (April 1980): 265-74.

Malvern, K. T. "The Effect of High Cognitive Questioning Techniques on Student Achievement After Teacher Retraining in Questioning Strategies." Ph.D. diss., Rutgers University, 1980. *Dissertation Abstracts International* 41: 04A.

Merwin, W. C., and Schneider, D. O. "The Use of Self-Instructional Modules in the Training of Social Studies Teachers to Employ Higher Cognitive Level Questioning Strategies." *The Journal of Educational Research* 67 (September 1973): 13-18.

National Education Association. *Questioning Techniques for Teachers and Students.* Sound filmstrip. Washington, D.C., 1984.

Pagliaro, M. M. (1978). "The Effect of Cooperating Teacher Questioning Behaviors on Facilitating the Questioning Behaviors of Student Teachers." Ph.D. diss., Fordham University, 1978. *Dissertation Abstracts International* 38: 12A.

Riegle, R. P. "Classifying Classroom Questions." *Journal of Teacher Education* 27 (Summer 1976): 156-61.

Riley, J. P. "Comparison of Three Methods of Improving Preservice Science Teachers' Questioning Knowledge and Attitudes Toward Questioning." *Journal of Research in Science Teaching* 17 (September 1980): 419-24.

Roby, T. W. "Models of Discussion." In *Questioning and Discussion: A Multidisciplinary Study*, edited by J. T. Dillon. Norwood, N.J.: Ablex Publishing, 1987.

Sanders, N. *Classroom Questions*. New York: Harper and Row, 1966.

Schreiber, J. E. "Teachers' Questioning Techniques in Social Studies." Ph.D. diss., University of Iowa, 1967. *Dissertation Abstracts International* 28: 02-A.

Showers, B. *Transfer of Training: The Contribution of Coaching*. Eugene, Ore.: University of Oregon Center for Educational Policy and Management, 1983.

Simon, A., and Boyer, E. G. *An Anthology of Classroom Observation Instruments*. Philadelphia, Pa.: Research for Better Schools, 1970.

Sparks, G. M. "Inservice Education: The Process of Teacher Change." Paper presented at the American Educational Research Association Annual Meeting, New Orleans, 1984.

Swift, J. N., and Gooding, C. T. "Interaction of Wait Time Feedback and Questioning Instruction on Middle School Science Teaching." *Journal of Research on Science Teaching* 20 (1983): 721-30.

Wade, R. K. "What Makes a Difference in Inservice Teacher Education? A Meta-analysis on Research." *Educational Leadership* 42 (January 1985): 48-59.

Walberg, H. J. "Syntheses of Research on Teaching." In *Handbook of Research on Teaching*, edited by M. T. Wittrock, pp. 214-29. 3d ed. New York: Macmillan, 1986.

Wilen, W. W. *Questioning Skills, for Teachers*. 2d ed. Washington, D.C.: National Education Association, 1986.

Zoch, R. F. "The Effect of an Individualized Inservice Program on Teacher Questioning and Student Verbal Participation." Ph.D. diss., University of Houston, 1970. *Dissertation Abstracts International* 31 (1971): 90-A.